ANIMAL ATLAS

For Juliette.
V. A.
For those who love animals.
E. T.

Published by Sourcebooks Jabberwocky, an imprint of Sourcebooks, Inc.
P.O. Box 4410, Naperville, Illinois 60567-4410
(630) 961-3900
Fax: (630) 961-2168
www.sourcebooks.com

Library of Congress Catologing-in-Publication Data is on file with the publisher.

Source of Production: Leo Paper, Heshan City, Guangdong Province, China
Date of Production: June 2016
Run Number: 5006856

Printed and bound in China.
LEO 10 9 8 7 6 5 4 3 2 1

ANIMAL ATLAS

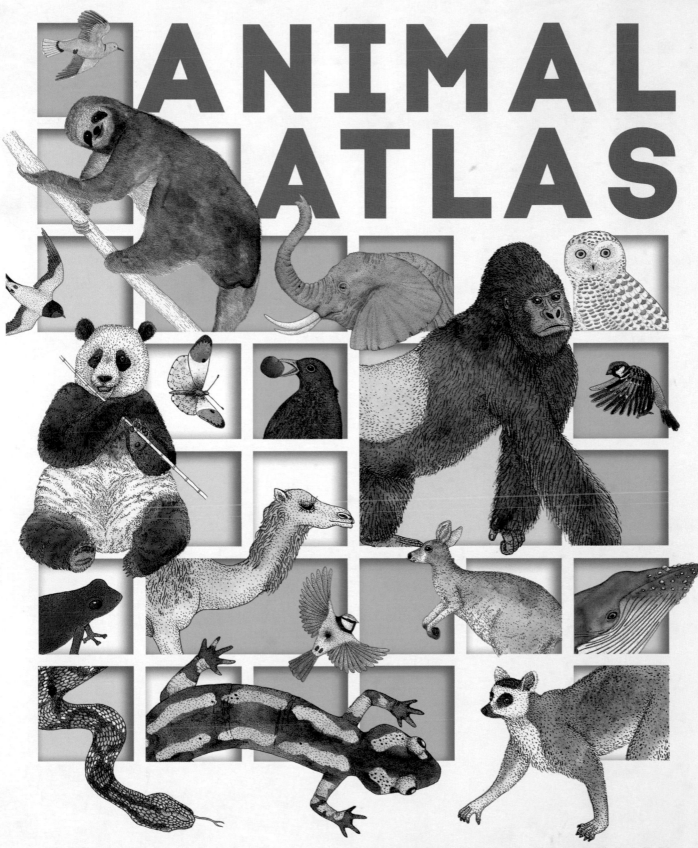

VIRGINIE ALADJIDI • EMMANUELLE TCHOUKRIEL

sourcebooks
jabberwocky

TABLE OF CONTENTS

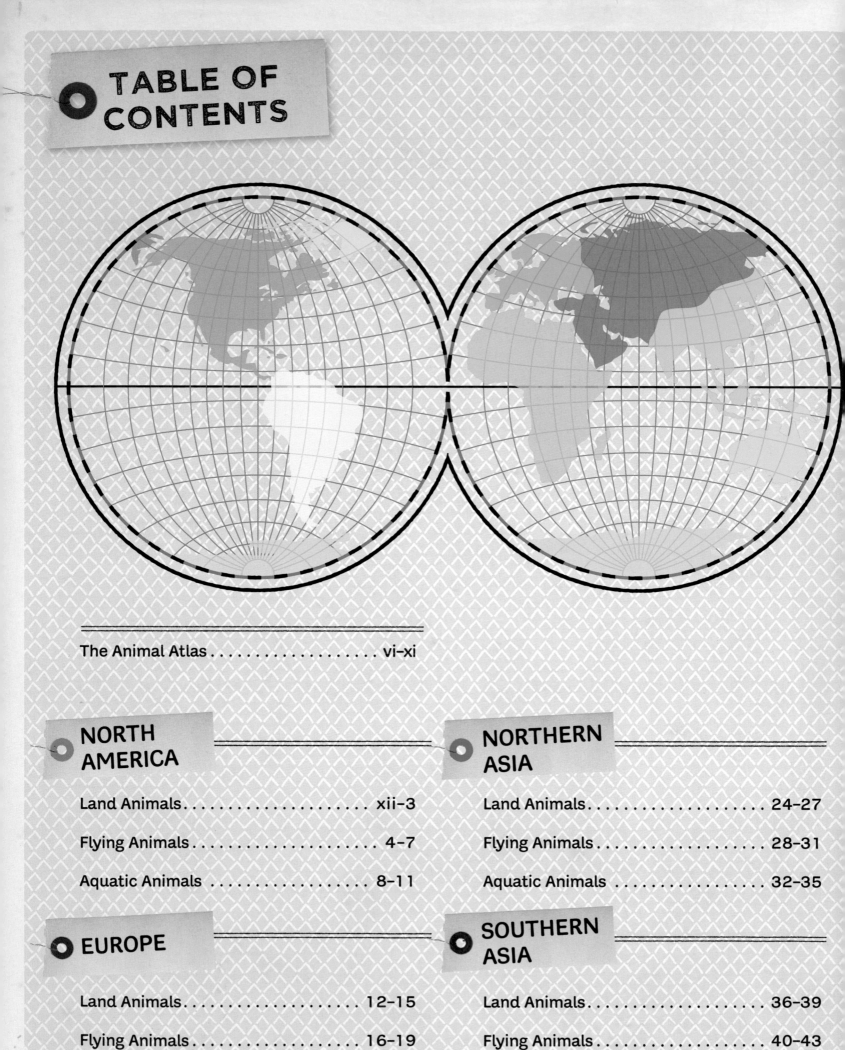

The Animal Atlas . . . . vi–xi

NORTH AMERICA

Land Animals. xii–3

Flying Animals 4–7

Aquatic Animals 8–11

EUROPE

Land Animals. 12–15

Flying Animals 16–19

Aquatic Animals 20–23

NORTHERN ASIA

Land Animals. 24–27

Flying Animals 28–31

Aquatic Animals 32–35

SOUTHERN ASIA

Land Animals. 36–39

Flying Animals 40–43

Aquatic Animals 44–47

AFRICA

Land Animals. 48-51

Flying Animals. 52-55

Aquatic Animals 56-59

SOUTH AMERICA

Land Animals. 60-63

Flying Animals. 64-67

Aquatic Animals 68-71

AUSTRALIA

Land Animals. 72-75

Flying Animals. 76-79

Aquatic Animals 80-83

THE ARCTIC

Animals 84-87

ANTARCTICA

Animals 88-91

Index of Animals 92-95

THE ANIMAL ATLAS

Children of all ages are fascinated by animals. Although the number of identified species existing on Earth is unknown, this animal atlas introduces nearly 250, including mammals, birds, insects, mollusks, reptiles, fish, and more. In this atlas, the world has been divided into nine zones. Each zone includes three maps that show:

- Animals living on land
- Animals that fly
- Animals that swim (freshwater and sea)

Emmanuelle Tchoukriel, an illustrator trained in medical and scientific illustration, drew each map and animal with precision. She used pen and ink to draw the black lines and watercolors to embellish the rest, which allowed her to play with shades and transparency.

Virginie Aladjidi is passionate about helping children discover a wide range of subjects, from nature to painting, and knows how to find the key to capturing their attention. She chose which animals and fun facts would be depicted for each geographic zone.

A Long Time Ago...

The five continents have not always existed as we know them today. Over time, they changed significantly by breaking apart and reforming. More than 1.3 billion years ago, one big supercontinent existed, but it eventually broke apart into several pieces. Then, 280 million years ago (during the Permian period), the eight pieces refused into one single continent, known as Pangaea.

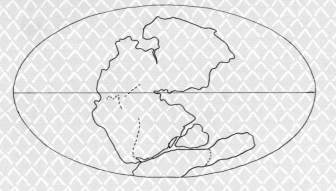

At the end of the Triassic period (200 million years ago), Pangaea split again, this time over a rift between North America and Africa, thus forming two continents: Gondwana and Laurasia. Similar fossil discoveries on multiple continents prove that they were once united. For example, fossils of the cynognathus (the ancestor of mammals) have been found in both Africa and South America.

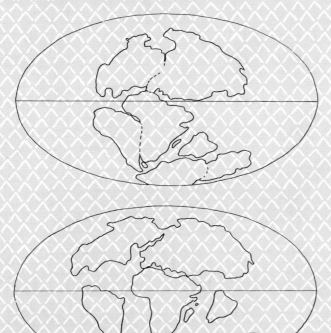

For the past 135 million years, the separation between the five continents has slowly become more pronounced.

Fauna Slowly Appeared on Earth

230 million years ago, there were small dinosaurs; mammals appeared 30 million years later. Birds evolved about 150 million years ago. Over millions and millions of years, species have appeared, and others have disappeared. Certain animals evolved very little, like nautiluses, whose shape has remained practically identical for more than 400 million years.

Dinosaurs disappeared 65 million years ago, and dodos disappeared by the end of seventeenth century. The scimitar oryx (an antelope) now exists only in captivity; they have been extinct in the wild since 2000. The eastern puma, also called the eastern cougar, was declared officially extinct in 2011. Today, more than 20,000 animal species are in danger of becoming extinct.

Animals and Their Habitats Today

Each animal has its preferred environment for food, temperature, survival, and reproduction. In each ecosystem, the animals, plants, and environment are all interdependent. The red macaw needs the heat of the tropical forest; the moose needs the forest's cold; the polar bear needs ice...

Certain animals are endemic: they only live in one area, like many of the animals in Madagascar, such as the ring-tailed lemur. Other species have spread out over several continents. These species either migrated to a similar environment or were "introduced," on purpose or accidentally, by humans.

For species that live in many areas, we have only depicted each species on two or three different maps to avoid repetition. For example, the house sparrow lives on every continent, but has only been mentioned once, in the section on South America. This allows us to explore a wider variety of animals within these pages.

(Drawings are not made to scale.)

Animals of the Prairies and Woodlands

Prairies exist in temperate zones, far from the equator. Many prairie animals dig burrows, to create a place to sleep since there isn't much natural shelter.

The European rabbit can be found in the prairies of Europe and Australia.

Grasslands also allow for raising livestock, like cows.

Animals of the Deciduous Forest

These animals live in temperate humid zones near the ocean where the seasons are clearly marked. The trees lose their leaves in the fall, then grow them back in the spring.

A wild boar eating the oak tree's acorns.

Animals of the Boreal Forest

The boreal forest, also known as the taiga, consists of conifer trees (trees with pine needles) and exists in the cold zones of temperate regions. Animals here have thick coats to weather the cold, and some hibernate through winter.

In Europe and Asia, the badger can be found living in the coniferous forests of temperate zones and the taiga.

Animals of the Poles and the Tundra

The Arctic tundra is treeless, but there are low-growing plants, mosses, and lichens, when the tundra is not covered in ice. Herbivores feed off these plants, and carnivores feed off the herbivores!

Animals, like the lemming, migrate to the tundra looking for food during cold periods.

Animals of the Mountains

Vegetation rarely grows on the mountains' rocks due to the wind and the cold. Animals living in the mountains are able to travel long distances to graze on sparse grasses or to hunt down their prey. Some hibernate while waiting for spring to arrive, which brings new vegetation.

The snow leopard, a large cat found in the high mountains, hunts jackrabbits and marmots.

Animals of the Tropical Rainforest

These animals live near the equator where the forest is dense, its trees reaching as high as 160 feet tall. The rainforest serves as a shelter for a wide variety of species.

Animals of the Savanna

In the savanna, very few trees can survive because rain falls only in the summer. The vegetation includes tall grasses and some scattered trees. Herbivores living in the savanna are hunted by carnivores, like the lion.

The savanna primarily exists in Africa. There, the baobabs grow wild and the zebus graze nearby.

The maki vari, or black-and-white ruffed lemur, pollinates the traveler's palm, a tree commonly found in Madagascar.

Animals of the Desert and Desert Zones

It hardly ever rains in the desert, making vegetation very scarce. Whether the deserts are extremely hot or cold and dry (like the Gobi Desert at an elevation of 5,184 feet), numerous animals manage to thrive in these extreme climates.

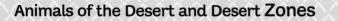

Warm water sea animals: corals, fish, and a sea snake.

Animals of the Ocean

Oceans cover 71 percent of Earth's surface and are inhabited by a wide variety of animals adapted to a wide array of environments: warm water, cold water, coastal water, foreshore (a zone between high and low tide), and the deep sea (far from the coast). To meet their food needs, sea animals live at various depths, from the water's surface to the dark, deep, cold abyss (13,000 to 19,000 feet below sea level).

The southern royal albatross, a seabird, can soar for a long time and swim; they have water-proof feathers and webbed feet. Some seabirds only set foot on land once a year to lay their eggs.

The meerkat and the fennec fox both live in the deserts of Africa.

The adventure is yours: turn the page and explore each continent, moving from the skies to the oceans and lakes to the Earth itself, as you discover the diversity of animal life...

NORTH AMERICA
Land Animals

American Moose

Western Diamondback Rattlesnake

Jaguar

Alaskan Husky

Brown Bear

Caribou

Gray Wolf

These can be found all over North America

Common Opossum

Appaloosa Horse

Ant Beetle

Least Weasel

American Bison

NORTH AMERICA

Land Animals

American Moose
Alces americanus
Class: Mammal

The largest of the deer species, the moose is the king of the boreal forest. Moose are as tall as horses and have a characteristic hump. They have dark brown fur with gray legs and big hooves that help them walk on soft snow or muddy ground. By plunging their heads underwater, moose graze on aquatic plants in lakes or wetlands. Moose are also found in Russia and Scandinavia, where they're known as "elk."

Brown Bear
Ursus arctos
Class: Mammal

Brown bears eat fruits, mushrooms, some small mammals, and lots of moth larvae. Mostly solitary animals, they congregate with other brown bears when fishing for salmon, snatching the fish up with their paws. During the winter, they seek out shelter in caves but do not hibernate. Subspecies of the brown bear are known as grizzlies, Kodiak bears, Syrian brown bears, etc., depending on the continent. (See also on p. 26.)

Caribou
Rangifer tarandus
Class: Mammal

Wild caribou herds can be found in Alaska, Canada, and the northernmost parts of the United States. The male and female both have velvet antlers used to defend themselves from wolves and bears. The antlers are red in the summer, but turn brown in the winter. (See also on p. 26.)

Gray Wolf
Canis lupus
Class: Mammal

The gray wolf prefers wide-open spaces, like those in Canada. Gray wolves belong to a pack of about thirty other wolves; together they hunt herds of herbivores or fish for salmon. Gray wolves are also found in northern Asia. (See also on p. 27.)

Western Diamondback Rattlesnake
Crotalus atrox
Class: Reptile

This snake gets its name from the ring-like segments at the end of its tail that make a noise like a rattle, warning its predators to stay away.

Alaskan Husky
Canis lupus familiaris
Class: Mammal

Valued for its strength, endurance, and extreme speed, the Alaskan husky, or husky for short, excels as a sled dog. They tend to be very affectionate dogs, bred to cuddle with other dogs as well as humans.

Common Opossum
|| *Didelphis marsupialis* ||
|| Class: Mammal ||

This nocturnal marsupial found only in
the Americas lives off of fruits and small animals.
Baby opossums remain in the womb for thirteen
days before they "climb" out into the mother's
pouch where they will finish growing. When fully
grown they are the size of a house cat. (See also
on p. 63.)

Least Weasel
|| *Mustela nivalis* ||
|| Class: Mammal ||

This little carnivore can climb trees to steal eggs
from a bird's nest. It can also poke its narrow
head into holes in the ground to search for small
rodents. Otherwise, weasels hunt birds and
amphibians. They can also be found in northern
Asia. (See also on p. 27.)

American Bison
|| *Bison bison* ||
|| Class: Mammal ||

Despite its enormous size, the American bison
can run as fast as 35 miles per hour. They live in
river valleys, and on prairies and plains. American
bison roam in herds, migrating in search of food.

Ant Beetle
|| *Thanasimus formicarius* ||
|| Class: Insect ||

Ant beetles can be found on fallen trees that still
have their bark, especially pine trees. They hunt
for bark beetles, flip them over, then pry them
open and devour them. Native to Europe, these
beetles were brought to North America to contain
a xylophagous, or bark-eating, insect population
called the scolytus.

Jaguar
|| *Panthera onca* ||
|| Class: Mammal ||

This large feline looks like a leopard but more
muscular. Its coat is marked by black spots called
rosettes (because they resemble the shape of the
flower). Jaguars live near tidal areas and in tropical forests, which are often flooded, where they
hunt tapir and deer.

Appaloosa Horse
|| *Equus caballus* ||
|| Class: Mammal ||

The Appaloosa, with its spotted coat, was brought
to America by the Spaniards in the sixteenth
century, then raised by the Nez Perce tribe near
the Palouse River, from which the horse gets its
name. The Appaloosa breed is popular for western riding competitions.

3

NORTH AMERICA
Flying Animals

Red Admiral
Butterfly

Red Cardinal

Golden Eagle

House Fly

Monarch
Butterfly

Bald Eagle

Razor-Billed Auk

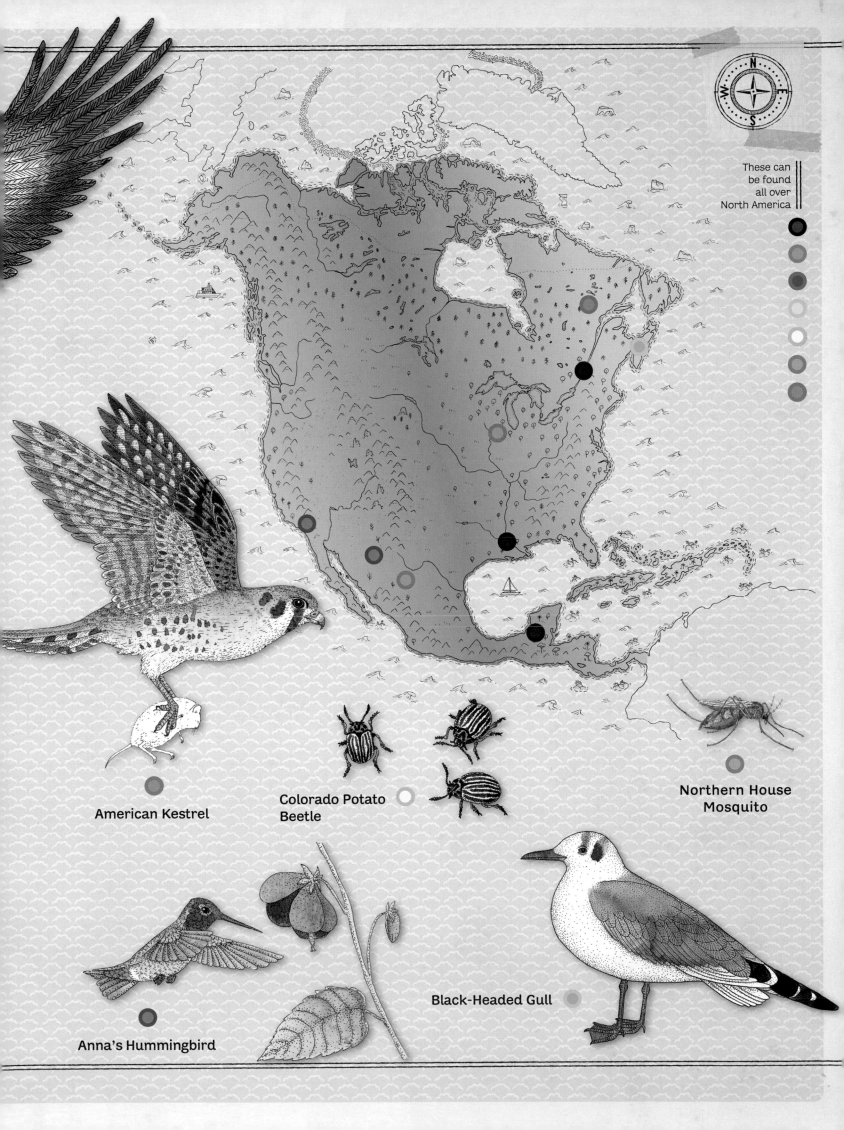

These can
be found
all over
North America

American Kestrel

Colorado Potato
Beetle

Northern House
Mosquito

Anna's Hummingbird

Black-Headed Gull

NORTH AMERICA

Flying Animals

Anna's Hummingbird

|| *Calypte anna* ||
Class: Bird

To seduce the female, the male Anna's hummingbird beats its wings quickly, swoops in the air, and makes a curious sound that results from the tail feathers rubbing together. The male can be spotted by its red head. Its long tongue is useful for gathering nectar from flowers, but it eats insects as well. They are also found in South America.

Monarch Butterfly

|| *Danaus plexippus* ||
Class: Insect

Millions of these orange butterflies with black veins join together twice a year and migrate 3,000 miles from the northern United States to southwest Mexico.

Black-Headed Gull

|| *Larus ridibundus* ||
Class: Bird

The black-headed gull, with its red-orange bill and legs, is native to Europe but has since migrated to North America and can now be found wherever there is a freshwater source nearby. They especially prefer lakes and ponds. (See also on p. 30.)

Red Admiral Butterfly

|| *Vanessa atalanta* ||
Class: Insect

The red admiral butterfly can have a wingspan over 6 cm wide. The larvae hang from certain plants—mostly perennial weeds, nettles, or pellitories—known as "host plants." (See also on p. 55.)

American Kestrel

|| *Falco sparverius* ||
Class: Bird

A small falcon that prefers open spaces and the outskirts of forests or cities, the American kestrel is cavernicolous: it makes its nest in tree cavities or muddy banks. American kestrels feed on insects, lizards, small mammals, and small birds. (See also on p. 66.)

House Fly

|| *Musca domestica* ||
Class: Insect

House flies have very short lives that span two to four weeks. Pads at the end of the fly's legs secrete a glue-like liquid between its hairs that helps it walk upside-down and on slippery vertical surfaces. House flies buzz or hum. Wherever there are people, house flies are almost always present as well. (See also on p. 31.)

Razor-Billed Auk

Alca torda
Class: Bird

The razor-billed auk's head is black in the summer, but white in the winter. They live on the rocky northern coasts of the Atlantic. Their wings allow them to fly quickly and also serve as flippers in the water. (See also on p. 87.)

Colorado Potato Beetle

Leptinotarsa decemlineata
Class: Insect

This flying beetle was discovered in the Rocky Mountains. It hibernates in a sheltered space and comes out during the spring. It hangs its eggs on the leaves of potato plants; the red larvae come out, then turn orange and bury themselves in the ground for ten to fifteen days before becoming fully mature. This beetle invaded Europe along with the introduction of the potato.

Northern House Mosquito

Culex pipiens
Class: Insect

Northern house mosquitoes have long antennae and the females possess a stiff proboscis that can pierce through skin, allowing them to suck blood, which is vital for laying eggs. Females only sting twice a week in the summer and once every fifteen days in the winter. The males feed on nectar and plant sap. (See also on p. 66.)

Red Cardinal

Cardinalis cardinalis
Class: Bird

The male cardinal has vivid red feathers stretching from its crest to its tail. It also has a red beak that crushes up seeds for food. The shape of its talons helps the cardinal perch on branches. Due to a highly developed syrinx (the organ that enables birds to vocalize sounds), cardinals can produce a wide variety of songs.

Bald Eagle

Haliaeetus leucocephalus
Class: Bird

This raptor, recognized by its white head and tail, lives only in North America and has been the symbol of the United States since 1782. A large predator of living prey, bald eagles also eat fish, both dead and alive. With a knife-like, yellow, hooked beak and sharp-clawed feet, the bald eagle is armed to kill. It has a wingspan of up to 8 feet. Eagles mate for life, but the male and female sometimes migrate independently before returning to their nesting ground and building a large nest, up to 20 feet tall, in a tree or on the ground.

Golden Eagle

Aquila chrysaetos
Class: Bird

Thanks to its long wings, the golden eagle can soar for hours, seeking out prey (deer, snakes, groundhogs, etc.), catching one between its sharp talons, and tearing it apart with its hooked beak. Along with other eagles, they can also be found in northern Asia. (See also on p. 31.)

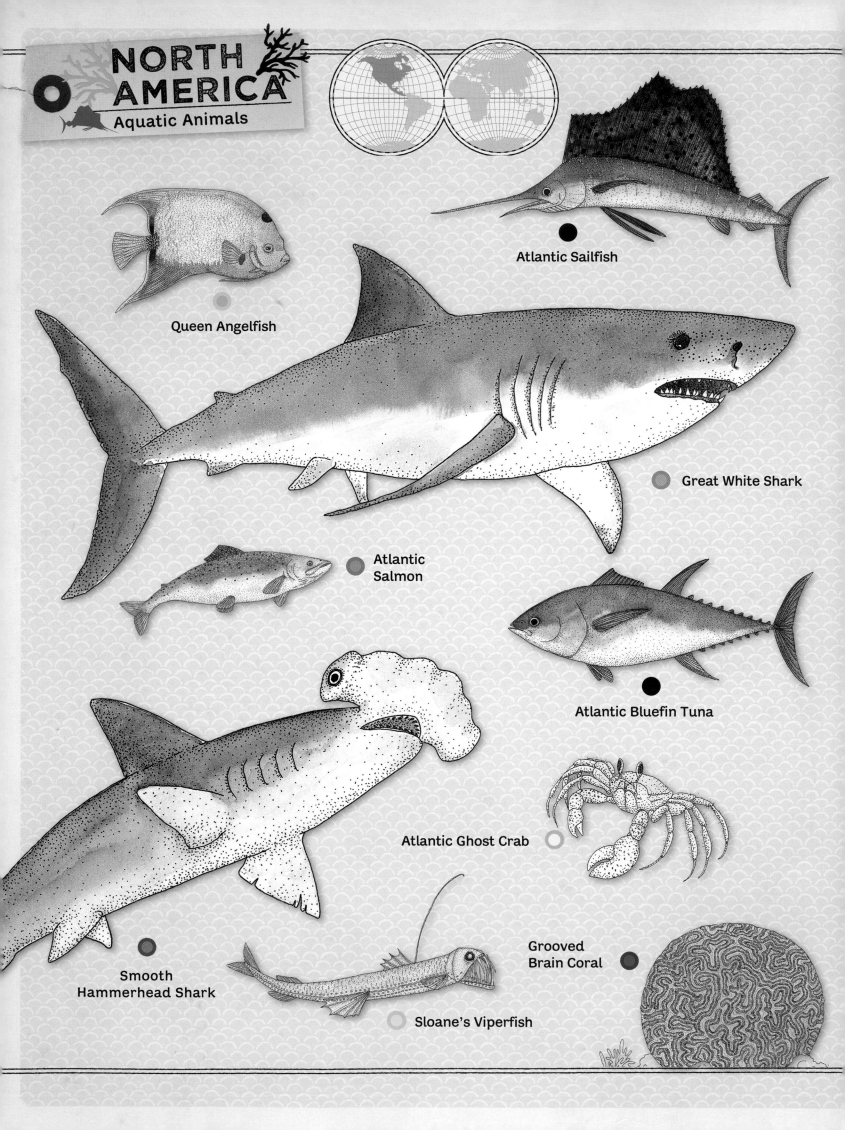

NORTH AMERICA
Aquatic Animals

Atlantic Sailfish

Queen Angelfish

Great White Shark

Atlantic Salmon

Atlantic Bluefin Tuna

Atlantic Ghost Crab

Smooth Hammerhead Shark

Sloane's Viperfish

Grooved Brain Coral

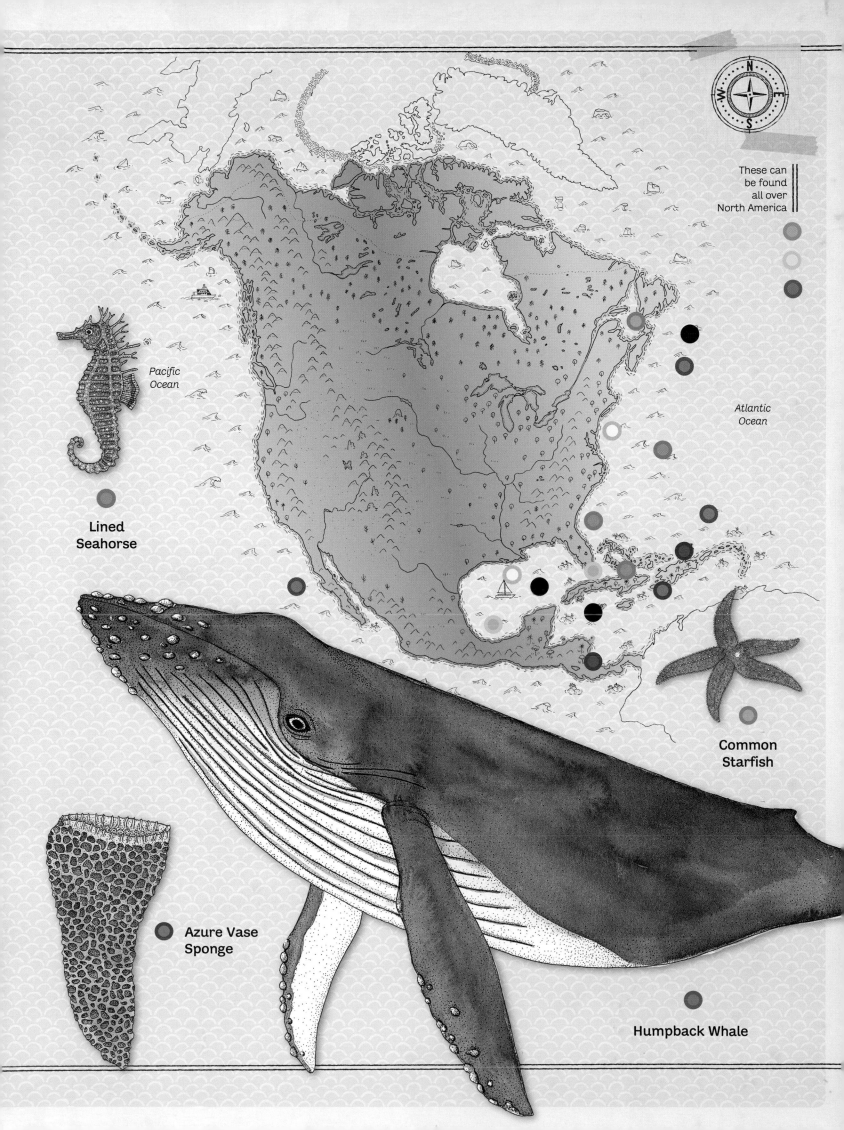

Pacific
Ocean

Atlantic
Ocean

These can
be found
all over
North America

**Lined
Seahorse**

**Common
Starfish**

**Azure Vase
Sponge**

Humpback Whale

NORTH AMERICA

Aquatic Animals

Grooved Brain Coral
|| *Diploria labyrinthiformis* ||
Class: Anthozoan

The grooved brain coral is a reef-building coral with a hard skeleton. It lives in harmony with microscopic algae, benefitting both organisms.

Humpback Whale
|| *Megaptera novaeangliae* ||
Class: Mammal

The humpback whale has a dark back and a white underbelly. It has growths called "tubercles" on its head and jaw, which are characteristic of the species. Its winglike flippers can be as long as 16 feet. They inhabit every ocean, including the waters of Antarctica. (See also on p. 90.)

Sloane's Viperfish

|| *Chauliodus sloani* ||
Class: Bony fish

This fish lives in the deep sea, 3,000 to 6,500 feet below sea level. Two lines of light-producing organs under its stomach and in its mouth help the viperfish navigate in the dark and send recognition signals for reproduction. (See also on p. 82.)

Queen Angelfish
|| *Holacanthus ciliaris* ||
Class: Bony fish

This West Indies fish has yellow and blue coloring. Its dorsal and tail fins extend out to a long, pointed tip. Like all angelfish, the queen angelfish's body is flat, like a pancake. They can also be found in the Pacific, Indian, and Atlantic Oceans. (See also on p. 70.)

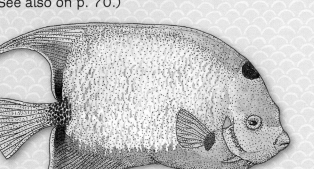

Atlantic Ghost Crab
|| *Ocypode quadrata* ||
Class: Malacostracan

This little crab gets the name "ghost crab" from its speed, disappearing as quickly as it arrives. One of its pincers is larger than the other. It is commonly found on the eastern coast of the United States.

Azure Vase Sponge
|| *Callyspongia plicifera* ||
Class: Demosponge

Solitary and often attached to a rock, the azure vase sponge can measure up to 50 cm high. Its appearance can be deceiving; it's not a plant, but rather an animal with a porous body. Like all sponges, the azure vase sponge feeds by filtering particles from the seawater.

Great White Shark

|| *Carcharodon carcharias* ||
|| Class: Cartilaginous fish ||

Great white sharks are excellent swimmers thanks to the back-and-forth motion of their crescent-shaped tail, which also enables them to jump out of the water. They're strong hunters, using their pointed teeth to tear apart their prey. They inhabit every ocean, except near the North and South poles.
(See also on p. 83.)

Lined Seahorse

|| *Hippocampus erectus* ||
|| Class: Bony fish ||

The male seahorse carries the female's eggs in a pouch on its stomach. Seahorses—whose name comes from the shape of its head—can swim upright using their small dorsal fin. They often anchor themselves down by curling their long tail around a piece of algae.

Atlantic Salmon

|| *Salmo salar* ||
|| Class: Bony fish ||

This silver fish is hatched in freshwater rivers. When it reaches the stage called "smolt," it moves to the sea, where it matures for a period of one to two years. The salmon then returns to its native river where it will spawn, lay eggs, and die. It is also found in South America. (See also on p. 70.)

Common Starfish

|| *Asterias rubens* ||
|| Class: Asteroidia ||

The common starfish has suction cups under its five arms that allow it to move around and to open and eat mollusks. If the starfish loses an arm, it will grow back!

Atlantic Sailfish

|| *Istiophorus albicans* ||
|| Class: Bony fish ||

With a body up to 10 feet long, this blue fish has a very pointed superior jaw and a long, flexible dorsal fin that propels it forward. The Atlantic sailfish has also been known to jump out of the water. At 68 miles per hour, it is the fastest fish in the ocean. It also inhabits the coasts of South America. (See also on p. 71.)

Smooth Hammerhead Shark

|| *Sphyrna zygaena* ||
|| Class: Cartilaginous fish ||

This shark, easily recognized by its characteristic snout, lives along the American coast in the temperate waters of the Atlantic. Out of the nine existing hammerhead shark species, only one is dangerous to man—this one is harmless! This one is harmless. It can also be found in southern Asia. (See also on p. 47.)

Atlantic Bluefin Tuna

|| *Thunnus thynnus* ||
|| Class: Bony fish ||

Excellent swimmers able to move as fast as 45 miles per hour, Atlantic bluefin tuna cover vast distances every day. Due to overfishing—their red meat is in high demand for food—they are now endangered. They are also found in South America. (See also on p. 70.)

EUROPE
Land Animals

Red Deer

Ardennes Draft Horse

European Badger

Chamois

European Hedgehog

European Rabbit

Red Squirrel

Wild Boar

Crested Porcupine

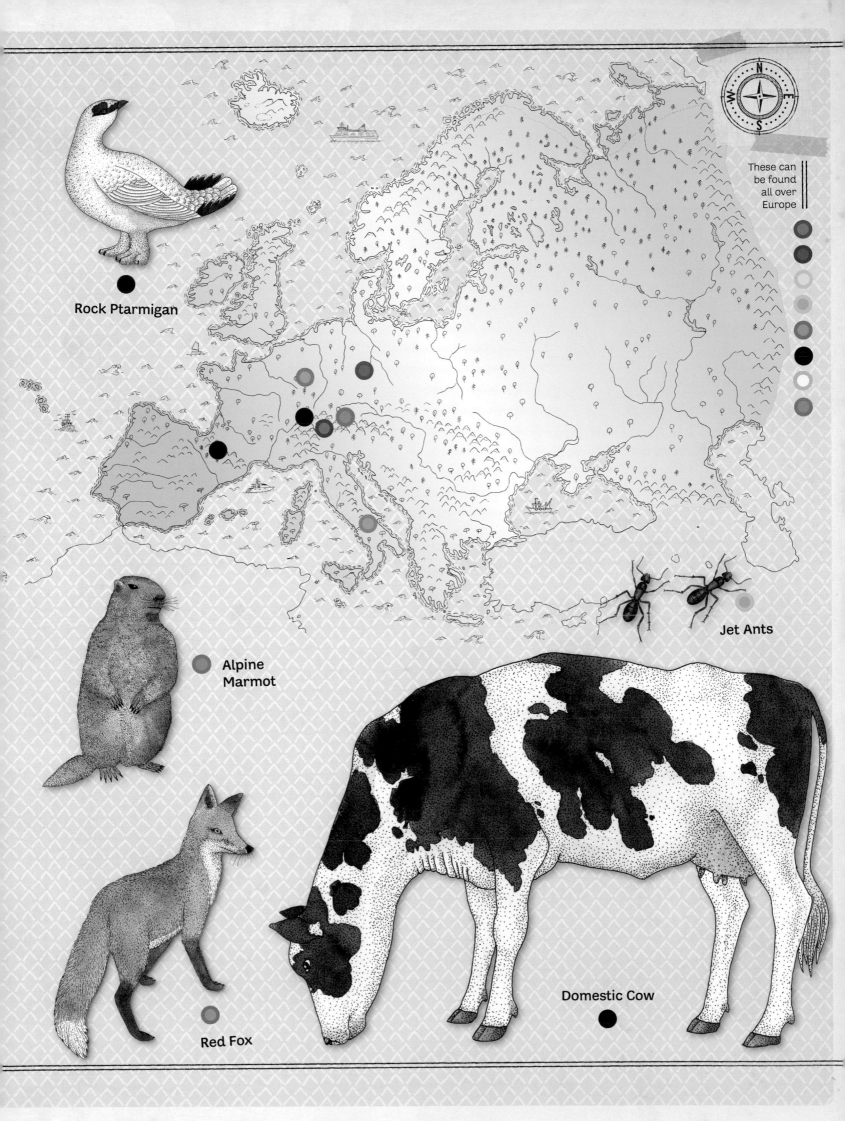

Rock Ptarmigan

Alpine Marmot

Jet Ants

Red Fox

Domestic Cow

These can be found all over Europe

EUROPE

Land Animals

European Badger
|| *Meles meles* ||
Class: Mammal
This animal, with black stripes along its snout, is an omnivore: it will eat mushrooms, rodents, frogs, insects, and more...it can even withstand snake venom! Badgers use their paws to dig tunnels; one burrow may have as many as thirty entrances and can be used by a number of badger clans over several generations.

Red Deer
|| *Cervus elaphus* ||
Class: Mammal
The red deer's coat is brown in the summer and gray-brown in the winter. The male is king of the forest, with its multiple-pronged antlers, though the red deer is smaller than its American cousin, the wapiti.
(See also on p. 27 and p. 39.)

Ardennes Draft Horse
|| *Equus caballus* ||
Class: Mammal
Heavy-duty, muscular horses, the Ardennes served as warhorses in ancient times to pull cannons and other military equipment. These domesticated horses now haul cargo. They have a brown coat and a black mane.

European Hedgehog
|| *Erinaceus europaeus* ||
Class: Mammal
A nocturnal insectivore with a narrow snout, the hedgehog hunts in parks or woods looking for insects, worms, and spiders. If attacked, it has 8,000 sharp spines to keep it safe.

Rock Ptarmigan
|| *Lagopus mutus* ||
Class: Bird
This stocky gallinacean, with feathers that turn white in the winter, has unique feet: thick and covered in feathers, they act like snowshoes on the snowy mountain ground. In the summer, their feathers are gray and brown. (See also on p. 86.)

Chamois
|| *Rupicapra rupicapra* ||
Class: Mammal
A nimble climber with horns curving toward its back, the chamois jumps from rock to rock—jumping 20 feet in distance and 6.6 feet high. Its hooves have a flexible pad that supports its movements in difficult terrain. Chamois eat mountain wildflowers in the summer and lichens or tree branches in the winter.

Wild Boar
|| *Sus scrofa* ||
Class: Mammal
The boar is one of the most widespread terrestrial mammals, living in many diverse habitats. With a barrel-shaped body, thin legs, small eyes, and snout on its large head, the boar is also the ancestor of the domestic pig. (See also on p. 39 and p. 74.)

Red Squirrel
|| *Sciurus vulgaris* ||
Class: Mammal
Mostly solitary, this rodent is an adept climber and eats nuts, buds, eggs, or seeds, found on the ground or in trees. Its fluffy tail is as long as its body, and its ears are furry, especially in the winter.

European Rabbit
|| *Oryctolagus cuniculus* ||
Class: Mammal
The European rabbit, or common rabbit, lives in colonies on the prairie and digs burrows for shelter. It cleans itself and can even turn its head around 180 degrees! Its incisors, or front teeth, are constantly growing. (See also on p. 74.)

Alpine Marmot
|| *Marmota marmota* ||
Class: Mammal
This large rodent, with four long incisors, which grow continuously throughout its lifetime, never wanders far from its burrow. The marmot runs on all fours when moving between rock piles and sunny meadows in the mountains, then stands upright to look out for danger, whistling if necessary.

Crested Porcupine
|| *Hystrix cristata* ||
Class: Mammal
Living in the mountains or desert, this large nocturnal rodent remains in its burrow during the day and is most active at night, looking for roots, insects, lizards, and frogs. Quills on its back serve as its defense mechanism. Native to Africa, the porcupine was brought to Italy by the ancient Romans.

Red Fox
|| *Vulpes vulpes* ||
Class: Mammal
With its slim profile and fluffy tail, the fox is active both day and night. It pounces on its prey, which usually consists of field mice or rabbits, then carries it away to eat in a secluded spot. The red fox also eats eggs, fruit, or garbage. It can live in the city as well as the country.

Jet Ant
|| *Lasius fuliginosus* ||
Class: Insect
Jet ants mix dirt, old wood, and saliva to build a nest in a hollow trunk or stump. They keep aphids (small sap-sucking insects) in order to feed off the honeydew (a sugary, sticky liquid) produced by aphids. The ants move by following the smell of each other's body odors.

Domestic Cow
|| *Bos taurus* ||
Class: Mammal
Cows are raised for their milk or their meat, depending on the species. In France alone, there are 19 million different kinds of bovines!

EUROPE

Flying Animals

Great Spotted
Cuckoo

Common Kingfisher

Great Black-Backed Gull

Barn Swallow

Common
Blackbird

Daubenton's Bat

Eurasian Blue Tit

Eurasian
Oystercatcher

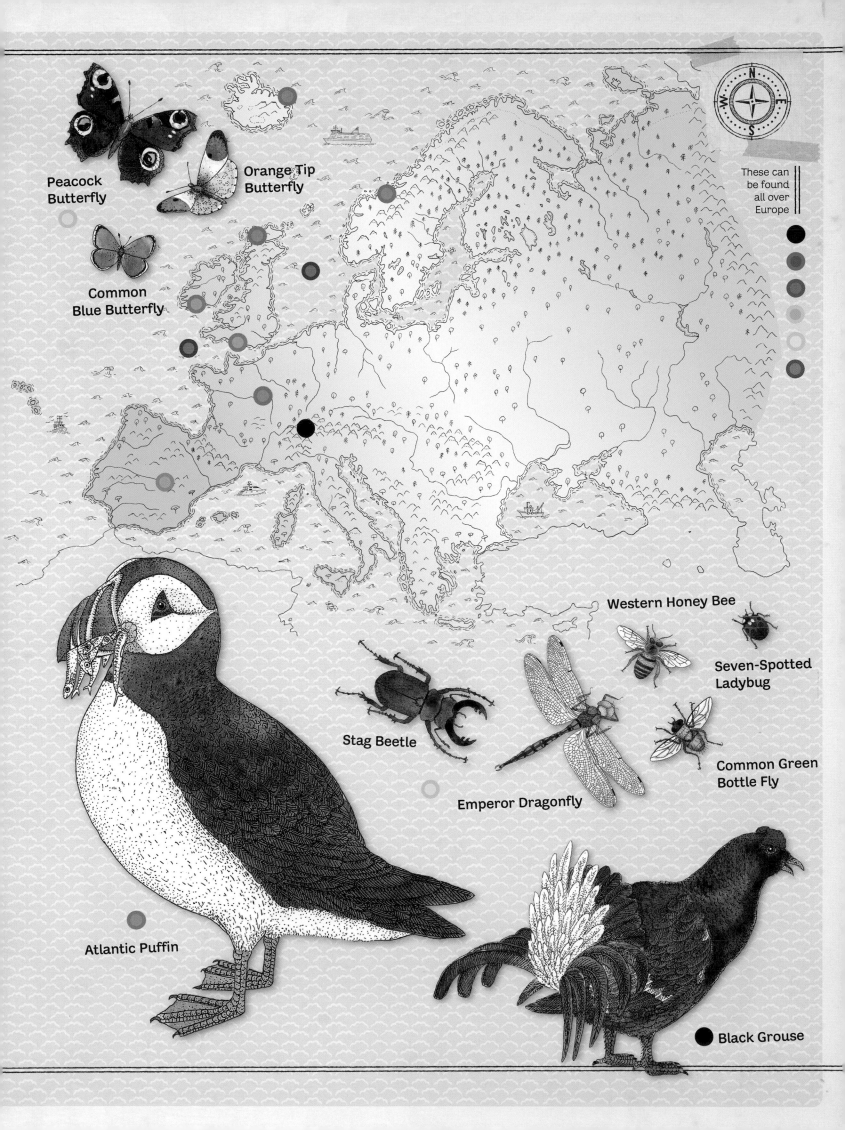

Peacock
Butterfly

Orange Tip
Butterfly

Common
Blue Butterfly

These can
be found
all over
Europe

Atlantic Puffin

Stag Beetle

Western Honey Bee

Seven-Spotted
Ladybug

Common Green
Bottle Fly

Emperor Dragonfly

● Black Grouse

EUROPE

Flying Animals

Great Spotted Cuckoo
|| *Clamator glandarius* ||
Class: Bird

This migratory bird flutters or hops around on the ground with its tail raised. Like all cuckoo birds, they lay eggs in other birds' nests. They often choose the crow or magpie as adoptive parents because their chicks have the same voice. Cuckoos are carnivorous and eat insects, mollusks, or small mammals. They can also be found in Africa. (See also on p. 55.)

Common Kingfisher
|| *Alcedo atthis* ||
Class: Bird

The common kingfisher, with its bright green-blue and orange feathers, lives near clear, shallow freshwater. It tucks its wings back to dive for fish, then knocks them unconscious on land before swallowing them. Also known as the Eurasian kingfisher, it lives in Europe and southern Asia. (See also on p. 42.)

Great Black-Backed Gull
|| *Larus marinus* ||
Class: Bird

The largest of the gull family (80 cm long with a wingspan reaching 170 cm), the black-back can be found on the entire North Atlantic coast. Its black wings, white body, yellow beak, and pink legs make it easily identifiable. It hunts in the sea and on land.

Barn Swallow
|| *Hirundo rustica* ||
Class: Bird

Barn swallows build a nest using mud and plants (mostly straw or grass) and garnish it with feathers to make it cozier. In late September, once they have finished raising their young, the swallows in France migrate as a colony above the Mediterranean and the Sahara, landing in Africa. (See also on p. 30 and p. 55.)

Atlantic Puffin
|| *Fratercula arctica* ||
Class: Bird

This migratory bird spends the majority of the year out on the open seas and can dive as deep as 200 feet to catch fish, which it either swallows immediately or carries in its bill to feed to its young. Spines covering the upper part of its beak and tongue allow the puffin to carry numerous fish in its mouth at one time! (See also on p. 86.)

Daubenton's Bat
|| *Myotis daubentonii* ||
Class: Mammal

This little bat flies several feet above the water while hunting for aquatic insects that it traps with its tail or feet. During the winter, they migrate far away to caves or mines where they will hibernate. They live in groups.

Eurasian Blue Tit

|| *Parus caeruleus* ||
Class: Bird
Blue wings, a blue crown, and a yellow belly characterize this little bird. The Eurasian blue tit lives in deciduous forests or gardens. In the winter, they hunt for eggs and insect larvae, which benefits farmers. Seeds are also a component of their diet.

Common Blackbird

|| *Turdus merula* ||
Class: Bird
A remarkable evening singer, this bird feeds on berries, fruits, worms, and insects. Their eggs are blue. The male blackbird has a yellow ring around its eyes.

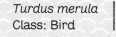

Eurasian Oystercatcher

|| *Haematopus ostralegus* ||
Class: Bird
At low tide, the Eurasian oystercatcher feeds on crabs or cockles (small clams), sliding its long, narrow bill between the shell's two halves to cut the muscle holding it shut.

Black Grouse

|| *Tetrao tetrix* ||
Class: Bird
This game bird lives in forests and mountain clearings. To attract the female, the male struts, displaying its fan-shaped tail.

INSECTS OF EUROPE
|| Class: Insect ||

Western Honey Bee

|| *Apis mellifera* ||
Bees live together in a hive of over 40,000 individuals. They make honey. (See also on p. 79.)

Emperor Dragonfly

|| *Anax imperator* ||
Originally from Africa, the emperor dragonfly is now one of the largest dragonflies in Europe (3.1 inches long).

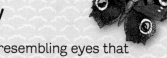

Seven-Spotted Ladybug

|| *Coccinella septempunctata* ||
This beetle consumes 150 aphids every day.

Orange Tip Butterfly

|| *Anthocharis cardamines* ||
The coloring of this species is defined by sex; the female's wings are entirely white, while the male's wings have orange tips.

Peacock Butterfly

|| *Inachis io* ||
This butterfly has spots resembling eyes that stand out against its ruby red wings.

Common Blue Butterfly

|| *Polyommatus icarus* ||
The top of this little butterfly's wings are blue for males and brown for females.

Common Green Bottle Fly

|| *Lucilia sericata* ||
This fly feeds on excrement using its proboscis, a short plunger-like appendage.

Stag Beetle

|| *Lucanus cervus* ||
This large, flying beetle is characterized by its impressive mandibles and can be found in the forest.

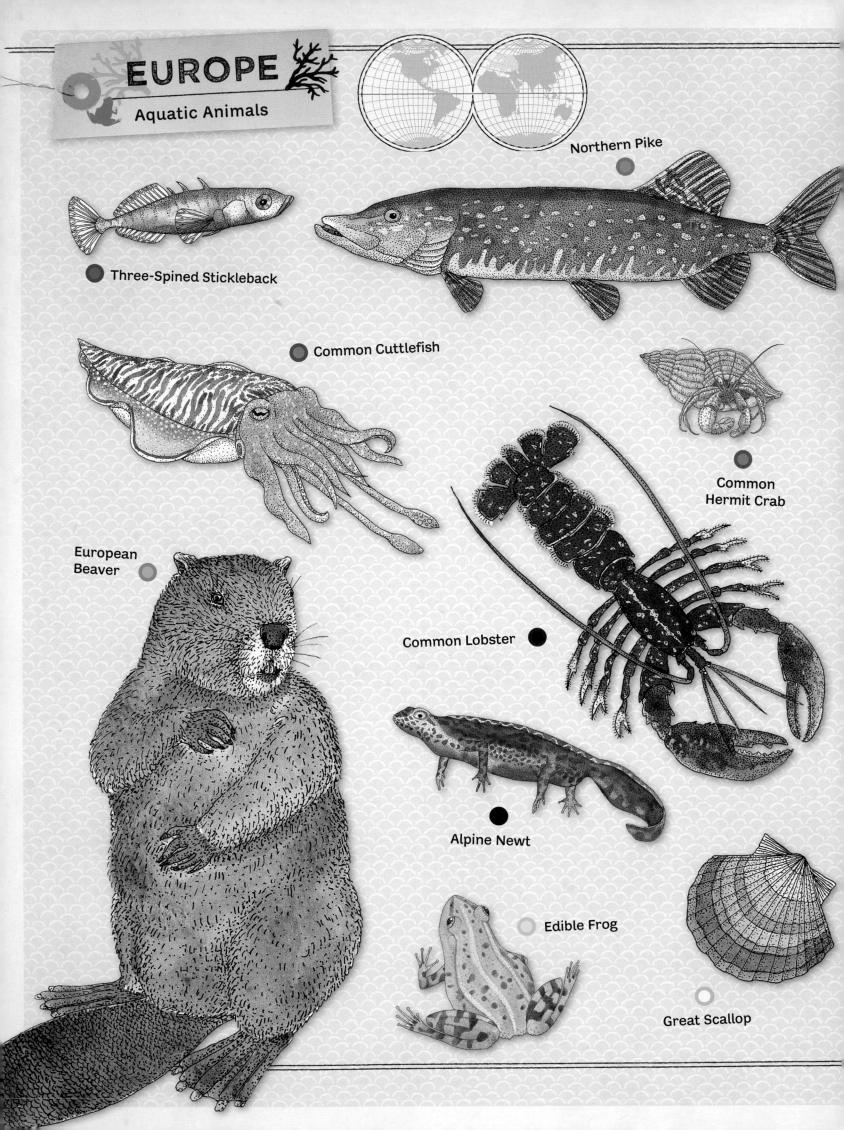

EUROPE

Aquatic Animals

Northern Pike

Three-Spined Stickleback

Common Cuttlefish

Common Hermit Crab

European Beaver

Common Lobster

Alpine Newt

Edible Frog

Great Scallop

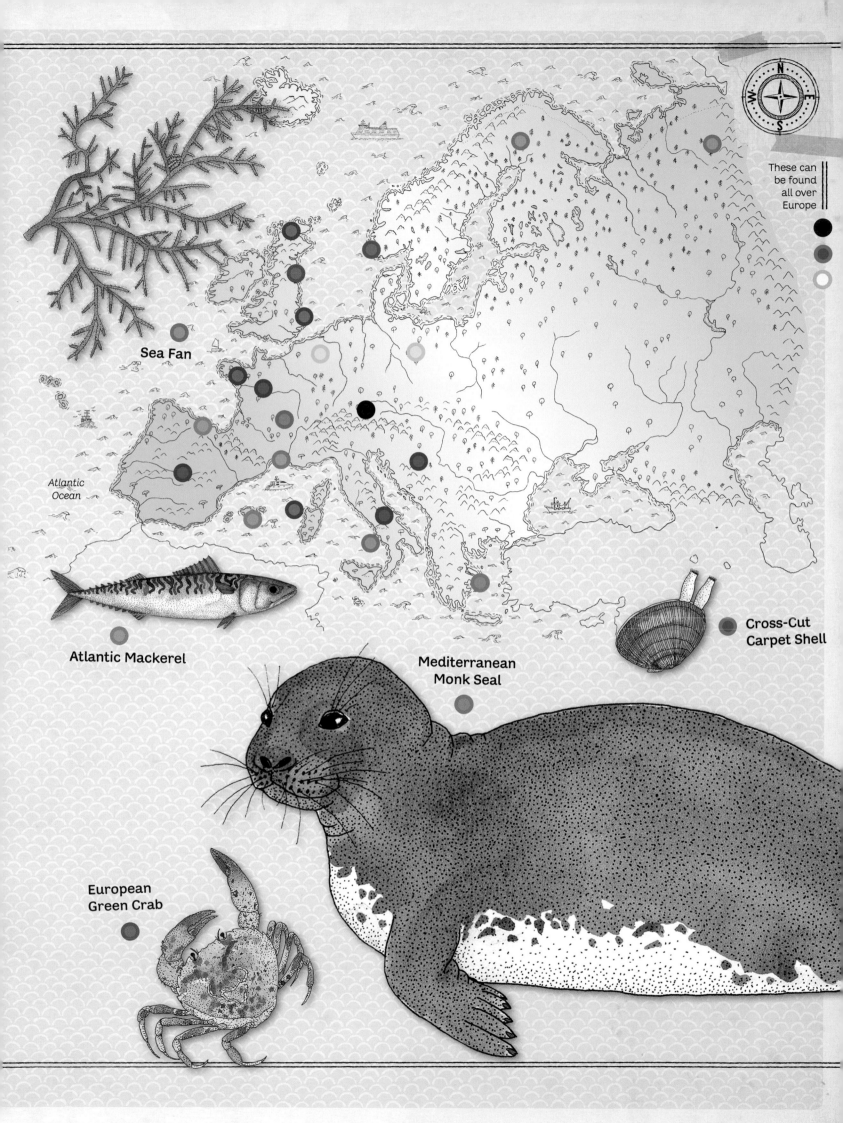

These can
be found
all over
Europe

Sea Fan

Atlantic
Ocean

Atlantic Mackerel

Cross-Cut
Carpet Shell

Mediterranean
Monk Seal

European
Green Crab

EUROPE

Aquatic Animals

Edible Frog
|| *Pelophylax esculentus* ||
Class: Amphibian

This frog can survive outside the water but comes to moisten its skin in freshwater on a regular basis. It spends four winter months hibernating in the mud. Its diet includes small crustaceans, insects, and worms.

Northern Pike
|| *Esox lucius* ||
Class: Bony fish

The pike is a very fast swimmer with one single dorsal fin. Its light colored stripes allow it to camouflage with plants in clear bodies of water and then catch its prey by surprise!

Three-Spined Stickleback
|| *Gasterosteus aculeatus* ||
Class: Bony fish

The three-spined stickleback's spines normally lay flat so as not to slow its swimming, but stand erect whenever a predator approaches. They can live in slightly salty waters (estuaries) or in freshwater (ponds or calm rivers). They are abundant in Europe.

European Beaver
|| *Castor fiber* ||
Class: Mammal

This large rodent can spend fifteen minutes underwater without breathing. The beaver has glands beneath its tail that secrete oil that makes its fur waterproof. Its flat, scaly tail is shaped like a paddle and acts as a rudder. The European beaver builds lodges and digs tunnels in riverbanks.

Common Hermit Crab
|| *Pagurus bernhardus* ||
Class: Malacostracan

This ten-legged crustacean has no shell; its body takes shelter in an abandoned shell, inhabiting new shells as it grows and develops. This species can be found on Europe's Atlantic coast.

European Green Crab
|| *Carcinus maenas* ||
Class: Malacostracan

The hexagon-shaped European green crab is one of more than 3,500 crab species in existence. Despite its name, the European green crab is not always green. Native to the shores of western Europe and Norway, they have been introduced all over the world by humans as a food source.

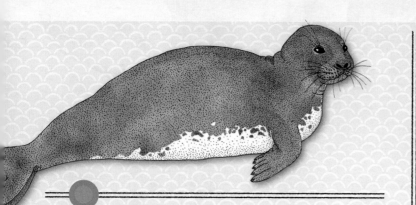

Mediterranean Monk Seal
|| *Monachus monachus* ||
|| Class: Mammal ||
This marine mammal dives to depths of 150–250 feet in search of food. The species is in grave danger of becoming extinct due to pollution and the destruction of its coastal habitat.

Common Lobster
|| *Homarus gammarus* ||
|| Class: Malacostracan ||
With one pincher for feeding and one for self-defense, these large crustaceans live anywhere from the continental shelf to almost 500 feet below the surface. It hides in its hole during the day and hunts at night. These lobsters can be found on the Atlantic coast and in the Mediterranean. Due to overfishing, they have disappeared from areas near ports.

Atlantic Mackerel
|| *Scomber scombrus* ||
|| Class: Bony fish ||
Recognized by the bands across its green-blue back, the mackerel lives in shoals in the deep sea, feeding mostly on zooplankton. It spends the summer in cold waters and migrates to warmer waters in the fall. (See also on p. 87.)

Cross-Cut Carpet Shell
|| *Ruditapes decussatus* ||
|| Class: Bivalvia ||
This clam with radiating lines on its shell lives burrowed in the sand. For food, it filters phytoplankton from the water using two siphons: one takes water in, the other sends it back out.

Sea Fan
|| *Leptogorgia sarmentosa* ||
|| Class: Anthozoan ||
Sea fans anchor themselves to the sea floor and live in colonies. They have stinging cells containing tiny, harpoon-like structures.

Common Cuttlefish
|| *Sepia officinalis* ||
|| Class: Cephalopod ||
The common cuttlefish lives in sandy shallow bottoms. They have eight arms, plus two tentacles used to catch prey. When alarmed, they squirt black ink.

Alpine Newt
|| *Mesotriton alpestris* ||
|| Class: Amphibian ||
Found living at altitudes as high as 8,200 feet, the Alpine newt spends it reproduction period living in ponds or other bodies of water. When it leaves the water, its skin becomes rougher, adapting to its new humid environment. Alpine newts are fast swimmers but move very slowly on land.

Great Scallop
|| *Pecten maximus* ||
|| Class: Bivalve ||
The scallop's shells are not the same—one side is curved, the other flat. The great scallop moves on the ocean floor by slamming its shells together.

NORTHERN ASIA

Land Animals

Gray Wolf

Garden Dormouse

Goat

Stone Marten

Reindeer

Brown Bear

Eurasian Lynx

Praying Mantis

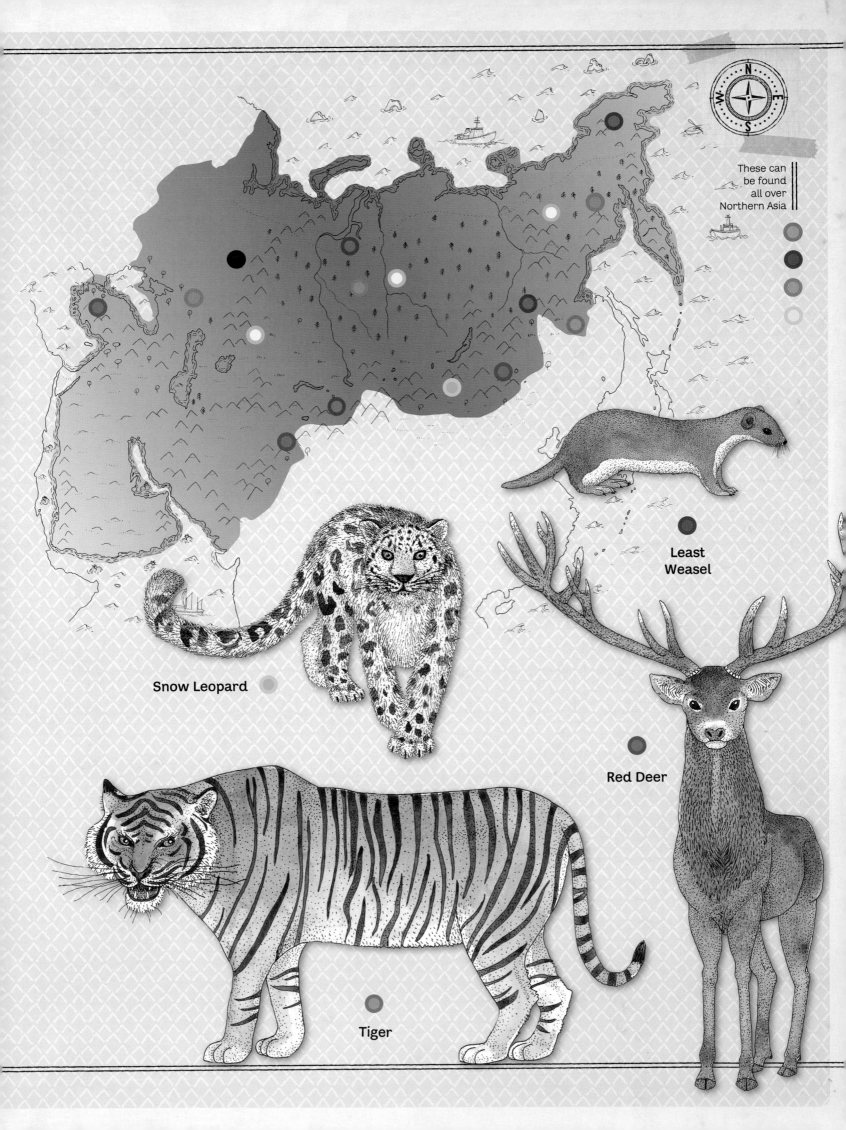

These can be found all over Northern Asia

Least Weasel

Snow Leopard

Red Deer

Tiger

NORTHERN ASIA

Land Animals

Snow Leopard

‖ *Panthera uncia* ‖
Class: Mammal

The snow leopard lives in high mountain ranges like the Altai Mountains in Siberia. To keep warm in the cold, it has dense fur with hair as long as 10 cm on its underbelly. It is nicknamed "the ghost of the mountains" because it is quiet and elusive and is considered an endangered species. They also live in southern Asia. (See also on p. 38.)

Reindeer

‖ *Rangifer tarandus* ‖
Class: Mammal

Living in the tundra or subarctic forest, reindeer migrate as the seasons change in order to find food. Their wide hooves enable them to swim and also act as shovels, allowing them to dig in the ground or under the snow to find weeds, bark, or lichens to eat. In North America, reindeer are known as "caribou." (See also on p. 2.)

Tiger

‖ *Panthera tigris* ‖
Class: Mammal

This large feline has a thick reddish coat with black stripes. They live solitary lives, hunting for deer and wild boar at dusk. Tigers are an endangered species and can rarely be found in northern Asia today. (See also on p. 38.)

Goat

‖ *Capra hircus* ‖
Class: Mammal

Goats' hooves allow them to venture across steep terrain. For food, they graze on vegetation. Humans raise goats for their meat and milk. Goats are on almost every continent!

Brown Bear

‖ *Ursus arctos* ‖
Class: Mammal

This large nocturnal carnivore can be recognized by its distinctive muscular shoulder hump and thick gray or brown coat. The brown bear needs a large area of land to survive. Its subspecies are known as grizzlies, Kodiak bears, or Syrian brown bears, depending on the continent. (See also on p. 2.)

Red Deer

|| *Cervus elaphus* ||
Class: Mammal

The red deer is an animal with a four-chambered stomach that lives in the forest. It is one of the largest deer species. They can also be found in eastern Europe (where they're smaller) and in southern Asia. (See also on p. 14 and p. 39.)

Gray Wolf

|| *Canis lupus* ||
Class: Mammal

Gray wolves live in wide-open spaces, like the Siberian steppes. They have incredible endurance and strong legs, enabling them to travel as far as 40 miles in one night! They can also be found in North America. (See also on p. 2.)

Stone Marten

|| *Martes foina* ||
Class: Mammal

This little brown carnivore is solitary and primarily active at night. Though they closely resemble pine martens, stone martens have white necks while pine martens' necks are yellow. Stone martens live in the country or in cities where they feed on garbage. They also search for eggs in chicken coops, which is why they're often viewed as pests.

Least Weasel

|| *Mustela nivalis* ||
Class: Mammal

Weasels look a lot like ermines, but they don't turn white in the winter or have a black tip at the end of their tails. Weasels can be found in North America as well. (See also on p. 3.)

Garden Dormouse

|| *Eliomys quercinus* ||
Class: Mammal

The garden dormouse, a little nocturnal rodent measuring 10 to 15 cm long (not including its tail), has facial markings that make it look like it's wearing a mask. They feed on fruits and insects, hibernating in the winter. Their main predators are cats and owls.

Praying Mantis

|| *Mantis religiosa* ||
Class: Insect

The praying mantis earned its name from the position of its spiked forelegs joined together as if in prayer. Its triangular head can rotate 180 degrees, allowing it to look directly behind. The females have been known to devour their male mates after reproduction.

Eurasian Lynx

|| *Lynx lynx* ||
Class: Mammal

This lynx is characterized by a small tail, long legs, and pointed ears that are crowned with tufts of fur. Largest of the lynx species, Eurasian lynxes also have long hair around their necks. A solitary predator, the lynx hunts for small ungulates, but never attacks humans. They can also be found in southern Asia.
(See also on p. 39.)

NORTHERN ASIA

Flying Animals

Barn Swallow

Northern Raven

Golden Eagle

Eurasian Collared Dove

Mute Swan

Snowy Owl

Green Hairstreak Butterfly

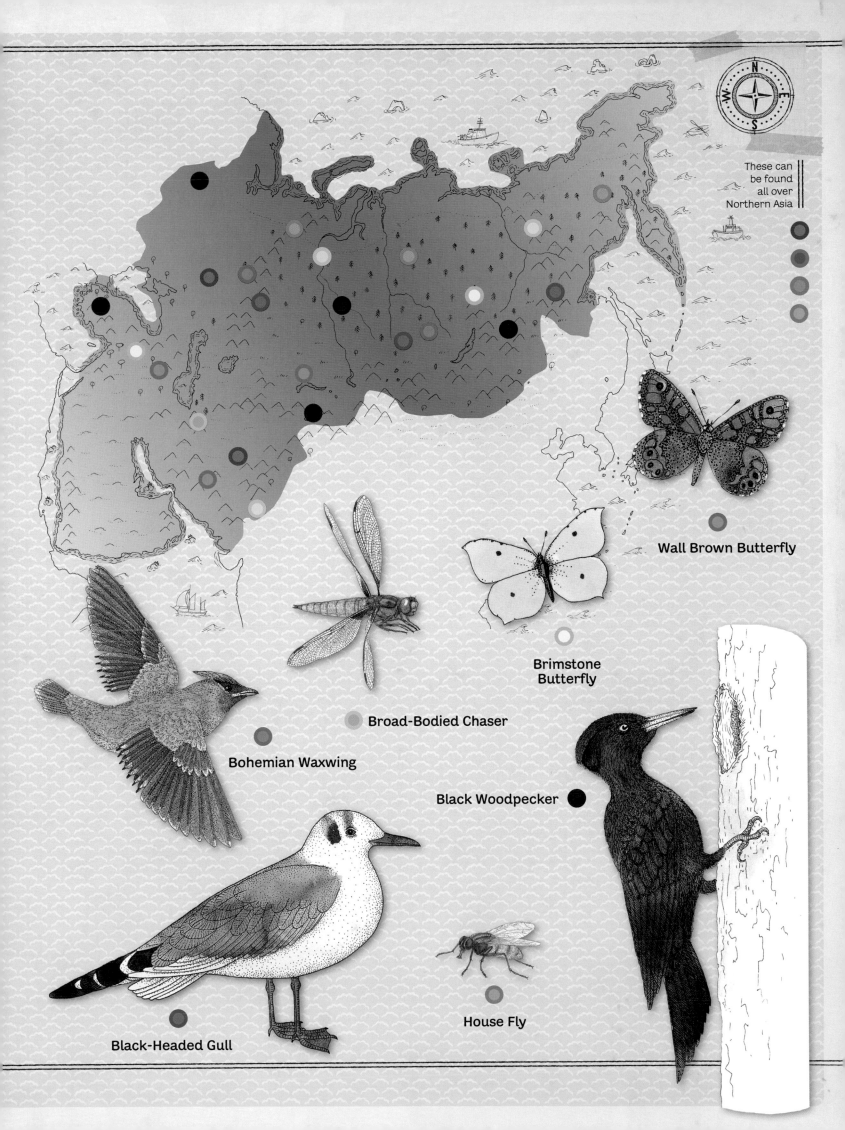

These can
be found
all over
Northern Asia

Wall Brown Butterfly

Brimstone
Butterfly

Broad-Bodied Chaser

Bohemian Waxwing

Black Woodpecker

House Fly

Black-Headed Gull

NORTHERN ASIA

Flying Animals

Northern Raven

|| *Corvus corax* ||
Class: Bird

The Northern raven is a large bird; those living in colder regions tend to be even bigger than those of Europe. They eat fruits, insects, and eggs, as well as decaying animals and garbage. They can live near humans but are most often found in the mountains. Ravens have distinctively shaggy feathers that stick out from the throat.

Snowy Owl

|| *Bubo scandiacus* ||
Class: Bird

The snowy owl's thick feathers cover up its legs and practically hide its beak. Not often found in flight, they are more likely to be found perched up high or on the tundra ground amid the mosses and lichens. The male is almost entirely white. Snowy owls also live in the Arctic. (See also on p. 87.)

Brimstone Butterfly

|| *Gonepteryx rhamni* ||
Class: Insect

The common brimstone butterfly's wings are shaped like leaves. The male is lemon yellow, while the female is pale yellow, nearly green. If captured, they "play dead." Brimstones live in the mountains.

Wall Brown Butterfly

|| *Lasiommata megera* ||
Class: Insect

Living in temperate zones, this butterfly is orangish-yellow with brown markings. On its wings, the wall brown butterfly has black spots resembling eyes with a light center. They often rest on bare surfaces to bask in the sun.

Black-Headed Gull

|| *Larus ridibundus* ||
Class: Bird

The black-headed gull's Latin name means "laughing gull," which comes from its shrill cry. These gulls closely resemble seagulls, but smaller. A black-headed gull is depicted here in its winter plumage: a white head and a dark spot behind its eyes. They can be found in most of northern Eurasia and in North America. (See also on p. 6.)

Barn Swallow

|| *Hirundo rustica* ||
Class: Bird

This bird has a long, deeply forked tail. In Russia, barn swallows journey over 6,000 miles as they migrate to countries south of the Equator. (See also on p. 18 and p. 55.)

Mute Swan

|| *Cygnus olor* ||
Class: Bird

The mute swan has a black knob atop its orange bill, known as a tubercle. Adults are white, while their young, called cygnets, are usually gray. Swans are able to swim and can feed on aquatic vegetation by reaching their heads underwater. (See also on p. 78.)

Broad-Bodied Chaser

|| *Libellula depressa* ||
Class: Insect

This dragonfly's scientific name comes from its broad and flattened, or "depressed," abdomen. The males are blue; the females are yellow. They are fast fliers and land with all four wings outstretched. They live near ponds or slow-moving waters.

Eurasian Collared Dove

|| *Streptopelia decaocto* ||
Class: Bird

The collared dove, with a black band around its neck, is known for its "coo," its well-known springtime song. These doves live in southern Asia and, since 1950, can be found in Europe as well. (See also on p. 43.)

Green Hairstreak Butterfly

|| *Callophrys rubi* ||
Class: Insect

This little butterfly's wings are brown on top and bright green underneath. Male and female green hairstreaks are identical. They're also very fast fliers.

Golden Eagle

|| *Aquila chrysaetos* ||
Class: Bird

This large brown raptor's dark eyes are able to see eight times better than humans can! The male and female mate for life. They build a giant nest in a high location then take turns sitting on the eggs (a maximum of four) for about forty days. Only one or two of the fledglings will survive. (See also on p. 7.)

House Fly

|| *Musca domestica* ||
Class: Insect

House flies live in close proximity to humans and can be found nearly everywhere on Earth. Their bodies, covered with tiny hairs, include a gray thorax and a striped back. The fly slurps its food through two spongy extensions at the end of its pointed mouthpart. If the food is too solid, the fly covers it with saliva to soften it up. (See also on p. 6.)

Bohemian Waxwing

|| *Bombycilla garrulus* ||
Class: Bird

The Bohemian waxwing has salmon-pink feathers, a sleek crest, and a black tail with a bright yellow tip. If a population hasn't gathered enough seeds at the end of a chilly summer, it will leave the coniferous forest as a group and fly up to 500 miles south of its traditional home. This massive exodus toward a non-habitual zone is called an "irruption."

Black Woodpecker

|| *Dryocopus martius* ||
Class: Bird

The woodpecker uses its black talons and tail to maintain a comfortable position while plucking insects from tree trunks with its long, narrow beak. They live in forests throughout Asia and Europe.

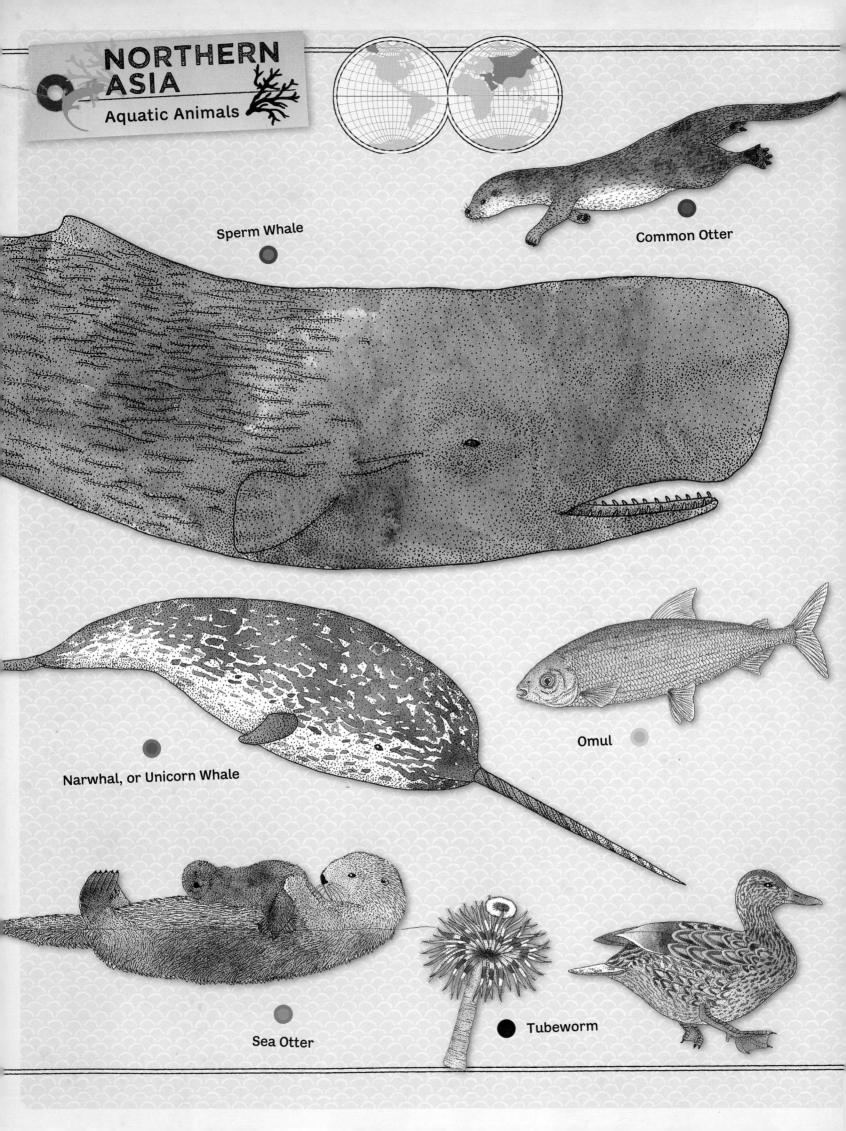

NORTHERN ASIA
Aquatic Animals

Common Otter

Sperm Whale

Narwhal, or Unicorn Whale

Omul

Sea Otter

Tubeworm

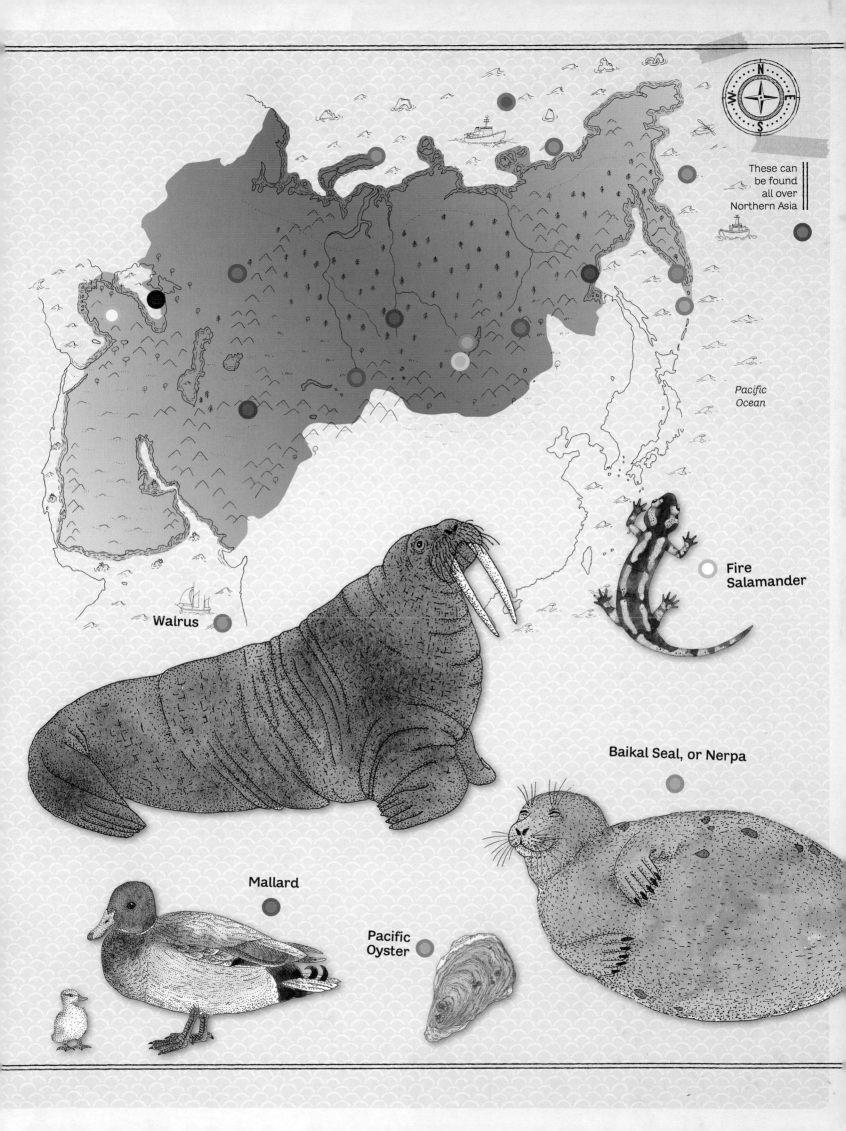

These can be found all over Northern Asia

Pacific Ocean

Fire Salamander

Walrus

Baikal Seal, or Nerpa

Mallard

Pacific Oyster

NORTHERN ASIA

Aquatic Animals

Narwhal, or Unicorn Whale

|| *Monodon monoceros* ||
Class: Mammal

With its large, twisted "tusk," the narwhal bears a striking resemblance to the legendary unicorn. The tusk is actually a tooth, which males (as well as 10 percent of females!) start growing around age 1. The tusk can measure up to 10 feet long. Narwhals can also be found in the Arctic. (See also on p. 87.)

Walrus

|| *Odobenus rosmarus* ||
Class: Mammal

The walrus can be graceful and aggressive underwater but is much less agile on land. Its growl can be heard from a mile away. In Asia, they can be found near the northeastern tip of Russia around the Bering Sea. They also live in the northern Atlantic and in the Arctic. (See also on p. 87.)

Baikal Seal, or Nerpa

|| *Pusa sibirica* ||
Class: Mammal

This silvery-gray seal with dark spots is the smallest of the seal family. It has claws for climbing on ice or rocks and a blubbery body that enables the seal to float in freshwater. In fact, the Baikal seal is the only seal able to live exclusively in freshwater.

Common Otter

|| *Lutra lutra* ||
Class: Mammal

Otters are excellent swimmers that hunt for fish and amphibians in lakes and rivers. When they get out of the water, they roll around in the grass to dry off. The otter's holt, or den, often has an underwater entrance, along with air vents.

Pacific Oyster

|| *Crassostrea gigas* ||
Class: Bivalve

This mollusk uses its gills to filter plankton, its main food source, from the water. It has a rough bivalve shell. Though native to Japan, the Pacific oyster is now present all over the world due to high demand for human consumption. Oyster farming has created many "ostreicultures," or cultures of oysters.

Mallard

|| *Anas platyrhynchos* ||
Class: Bird

Male mallards have colorful feathers during the breeding period, while females remain brown and beige. They are good swimmers thanks to their webbed feet and can stay dry due to the oil secreted near their tails; from a very young age, mallards use their bills to spread this oil and waterproof their feathers. (See also on p. 78.)

Omul

|| *Coregonus migratorius* ||
Class: Bony fish

Over 52 fish species have been identified in Lake Baikal. The omul is one of the lake's endemic species; it cannot be found anywhere else. With silvery sides and a darker back, the omul is commonly consumed in Russia.

Sea Otter

|| *Enhydra lutris* ||
Class: Mammal

The sea otter is the smallest marine mammal. Sea otters have dense, thick fur adapted to the ocean's cold water and are known for floating on their backs, especially when sleeping or sheltering their young. (See also on p. 47.)

Fire Salamander

|| *Salamandra salamandra* ||
Class: Amphibian

The female salamander deposits larvae in a shallow body of water. Once the salamanders mature into adults, they can no longer swim. They live in humid environments and forage for food at night.

Tubeworm

|| *Serpula vermicularis* ||
Class: Polychaeta

This worm lives in a self-constructed calcareous tube. At high tide, its featherlike retractable red tentacles come out, while at low tide, a special funnel-shaped tentacle with a serrated edge acts like a plug and closes the tube's opening.

Sperm Whale

|| *Physeter macrocephalus* ||
Class: Mammal

This large predator's brain is more than five times heavier than a human's. Sperm whales require between 1,000 lbs. and 1.5 tons of food each day. They can also be found in the southern Pacific and the Arctic. (See also on p. 35 and p. 82.)

SOUTHERN ASIA

Land Animals

Tiger

Bornean Orangutan

Red Imported
Fire Ant

Snow
Leopard

Red Deer

Wild Boar

Asian Elephant

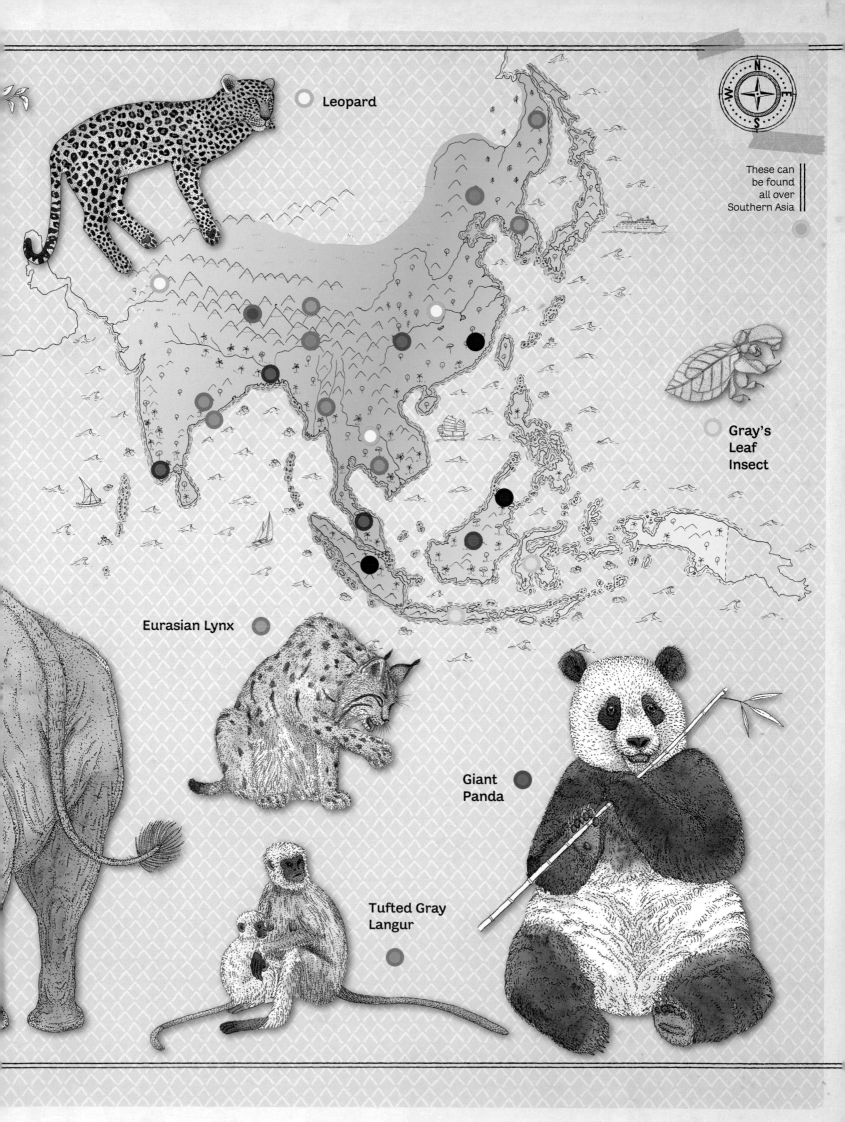

Leopard

These can
be found
all over
Southern Asia

Gray's
Leaf
Insect

Eurasian Lynx

Giant
Panda

Tufted Gray
Langur

SOUTHERN ASIA

Land Animals

Red Imported Fire Ant

|| *Solenopsis invicta* ||
Class: Insect

These red ants don't bite, but they do sting; the ant uses its mandibles to firmly latch on to its victim before sinking in its stinger. The first ant to attack releases a chemical substance called a pheromone that attracts the other ants to come attack the victim as well. Red imported fire ants originated in South America but can now be found in Australia as well. (See also on p. 63 and p. 75.)

Giant Panda

|| *Ailuropoda melanoleuca* ||
Class: Mammal

Measuring 4 to 6 feet long, the giant panda is only found in the high altitude forests of central China. In addition to its five fingers, the panda has a "false thumb" used for grasping bamboo shoots, its dietary staple. However, the panda's digestive tract is not adapted to its vegetarian diet, thus classifying it as carnivorous—and on occasion, it will eat decaying animals or small rodents. Deforestation is destroying bamboo forests, consequently reducing the giant panda population.

Leopard

|| *Panthera pardus* ||
Class: Mammal

This majestic feline has a spotted coat that serves as camouflage. Asiatic leopards are slightly lighter in color than the same species in Africa. The black leopard—generally known as the "black panther"—has black spots on a black background and lives in the rainforests of Asia. (See also on p. 50.)

Snow Leopard

|| *Panthera uncia* ||
Class: Mammal

Living in high mountains like the Himalayas, this beautiful feline spends the summer hunting yak and mouflon (mountain sheep), as well as smaller prey such as marmots and hares. In the winter, snow leopards attack deer and wild boar in the forest. They can also be found in northern Asia. (See also on p. 26.)

Tufted Gray Langur

|| *Semnopithecus priam* ||
Class: Mammal

This little monkey has a black face surrounded by grayish-white hair. Gray langurs live in trees and feed mostly on leaves.

Tiger

|| *Panthera tigris* ||
Class: Mammal

The tiger, with its black and orange stripes, is the largest cat in the world—even bigger than the lion. In the past, tigers could be found all over Asia, but now only about 3,100 remain. The most concentrated tiger population is in the tropical forests of India. (See also on p. 26.)

Wild Boar

Sus scrofa
Class: Mammal

The facial area including the wild boar's nose and mouth is called a "snout." Its bristles, or coarse hairs, are used to make hairbrushes. In the forests of southeast Asia, the wild boar is the main food source for tigers. They are widely distributed around the globe; for example, they can also be found in Europe and Australia. (See also on p. 15 and p. 74.)

Bornean Orangutan

Pongo pygmaeus
Class: Mammal

In Malaysian, "orangutan" means "person of the forest." Orangutans are roughly the size of a twelve-year-old child and belong to the hominid family, which also includes bonobos, chimpanzees, gorillas, and humans. They are primarily arboreal, meaning they live and nest in the trees, and their diet consists of fruit, eggs, and insects. The females take care of their young for at least three years, carrying them on her stomach or back. The males often live in solitude, but their calls can be heard from half a mile away.

Eurasian Lynx

Lynx lynx
Class: Mammal

The Eurasian lynx is the largest of the lynxes. Its wide paws act like snowshoes on the snow. They are particularly common in northern Asia but can also be found in the forests of China. For food, they hunt small deer. (See also on p. 27.)

Red Deer

Cervus elaphus
Class: Mammal

Female deer are known as "does" and their young are called "fawns." The males, generally darker in color, grow new coats twice a year: their coats are thin in the spring, then molt to a thicker coat in the fall to prepare for colder weather. The male and female both have a yellowish spot near the tail known as a "rump patch." Red deer can also be found in eastern Europe and northern Asia. (See also on p. 14 and p. 27.)

Gray's Leaf Insect

Phyllium bioculatum
Class: Insect

Known as leaf insects for a reason, the Gray's leaf insect is remarkably well camouflaged. There are over thirty leaf insect species in the world. They are concentrated in India, Indonesia, the Seychelles, and the warm regions of Australia. The females have wings, but are unable to fly.

Asian Elephant

Elephas maximus
Class: Mammal

Asian elephants have smaller ears and are smaller in size than their African cousin. Their heads also have two distinctive bumps, or domes. As herbivores, they forage in the forest and are particularly fond of the durian, a tree with foul-smelling fruit.

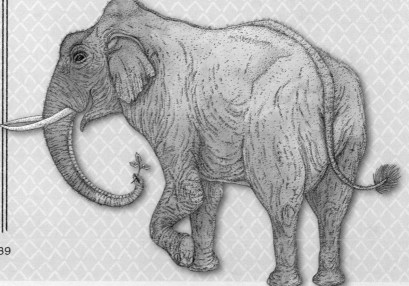

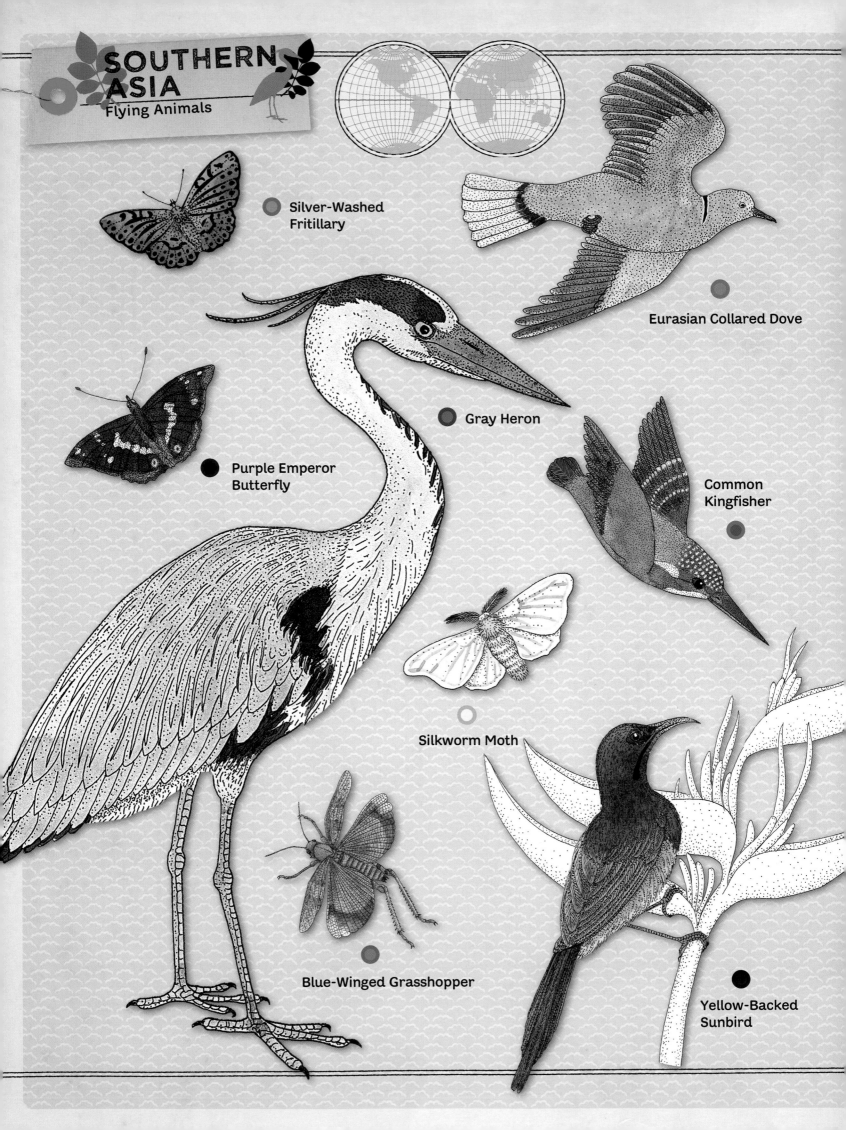

SOUTHERN ASIA
Flying Animals

Silver-Washed Fritillary

Eurasian Collared Dove

Gray Heron

Purple Emperor Butterfly

Common Kingfisher

Silkworm Moth

Blue-Winged Grasshopper

Yellow-Backed Sunbird

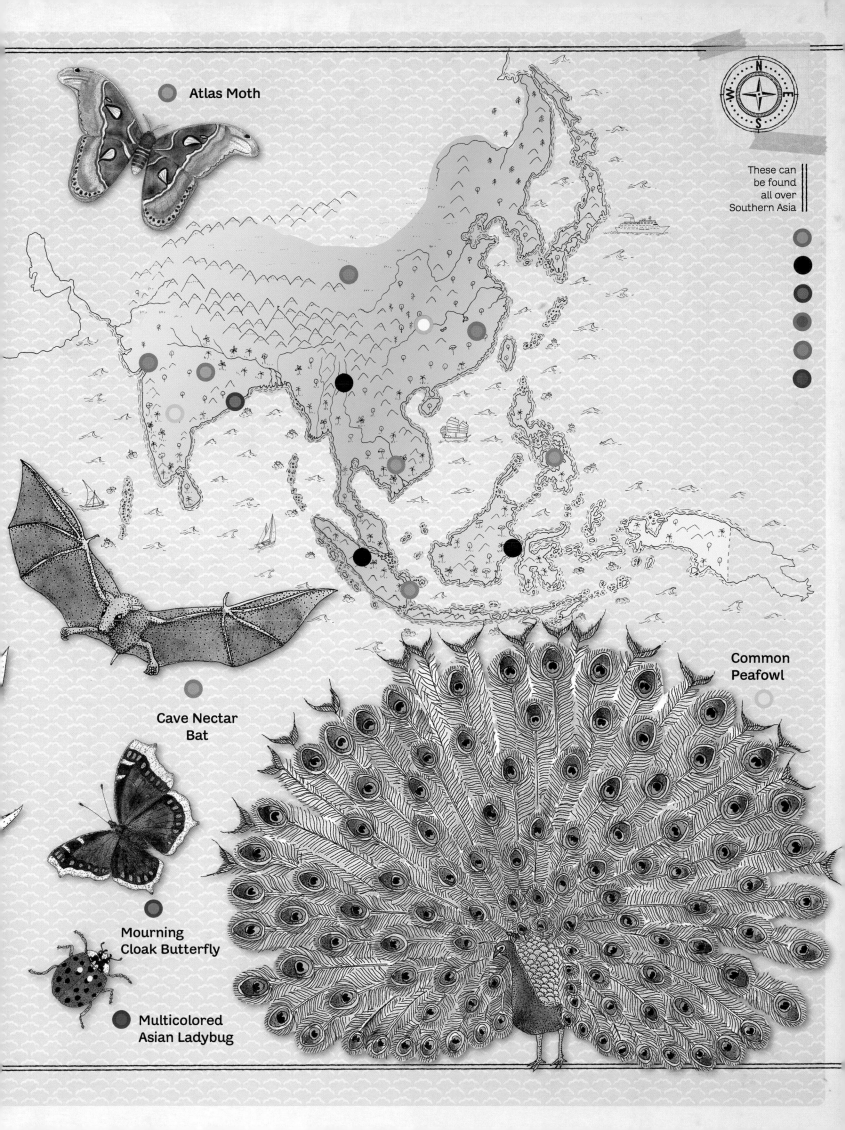

Atlas Moth

These can
be found
all over
Southern Asia

**Common
Peafowl**

**Cave Nectar
Bat**

**Mourning
Cloak Butterfly**

**Multicolored
Asian Ladybug**

SOUTHERN ASIA

Flying Animals

Yellow-Backed Sunbird
|| *Aethopyga siparaja* ||
Class: Bird

The yellow-backed sunbird is a singing bird with a distinctive crimson-red neck found in India, Indonesia, and the Philippines. The sunbird mostly feeds on flower nectar that it harvests through its long, down-curved bill. Its Latin name, meaning "crimson sunbird," comes from the way the male's iridescent plumage reflects the light.

Common Peafowl
|| *Pavo cristatus* ||
Class: Bird

Native to Asia, the male peafowl—known as the peacock—is easily distinguished by its blue body and long train of feathers, each tipped with vibrant spots resembling eyes. The peacock displays its feathers to attract the peahen. Peafowl are able to fly, even with their long trains, but mostly prefer to stay on the ground.

Common Kingfisher
|| *Alcedo atthis* ||
Class: Bird

Though common in Europe, the kingfisher is also widespread in southern Asia and makes its burrow in riverbanks. Fishing is its principal activity; the kingfisher can spot its prey from almost one hundred yards away! (See also on p. 18.)

Silver-Washed Fritillary
|| *Argynnis paphia* ||
Class: Insect

The silver-washed fritillary is a large butterfly whose orange wings are speckled with black spots. Additionally, the males have black stripes. They live in clearings, and the caterpillars feed on violets.

Mourning Cloak Butterfly
|| *Nymphalis antiopa* ||
Class: Insect

Recognized by its brown wings bordered with blue spots and a pale yellow edge, this large butterfly has become rare. It lives in Europe, North America, Australia, and Madagascar. (See also on p. 78.)

Blue-Winged Grasshopper
|| *Oedipoda caerulescens* ||
Class: Insect

This grasshopper can be found in areas with low vegetation. When its wings are folded, it blends in with the ground, but when it flies or jumps, it shows off a pair of brilliant blue hind wings. Blue-winged grasshoppers are thermophilic insects, meaning they prefer dry, sunny places. The male sings during the day to attract females.

Cave Nectar Bat

|| *Eonycteris spelaea* ||
Class: Mammal

This Asiatic bat plays an important role by pollinating many fruit trees during the six-week period when their flowers are in bloom. Cave nectar bats' natural habitat, the mangrove forest, is disappearing. This threatens not only the bats' survival but also the trees' ability to produce fruit.

Purple Emperor Butterfly

|| *Apatura iris* ||
Class: Insect

Large and dark, the purple emperor has white bands on its wing in the shape of a V. Males are a shiny bluish color, while the females are brown. They spend much of their time in the trees, especially willows, poplars, oaks, and orchards.

Silkworm Moth

|| *Bombyx mori* ||
Class: Insect

Silkworm moths are white with triangular wings. They lay their eggs on white mulberry leaves, the caterpillar's preferred food. When entering the transition phase from caterpillar to moth, they're protected by a cocoon of silk; each cocoon is made up of one single silk thread (around 3,000 feet long)!

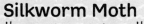

Multicolored Asian Ladybug

|| *Harmonia axyridis* ||
Class: Insect

This large ladybug native to China varies in color, ranging from red-orange and yellow to black. They were introduced to Europe to control aphids, their main food source, but they've also harmed tender grapes and the larvae of other European ladybugs, like the seven-spotted ladybug.

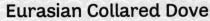

Atlas Moth

|| *Attacus atlas* ||
Class: Insect

This nocturnal Asiatic moth is considered one of the largest moths in the world, alongside the comet moth of Madagascar. They are also called the "snake's head moth" after the shape and coloration of the outer tips of their wings. The male's feathery antennae are wider than the female's.

Eurasian Collared Dove

|| *Streptopelia decaocto* ||
Class: Bird

The male and female both have the same black half-collar around the neck. They feed on seeds, buds, and berries. The Eurasian collared dove can also be found in northern Asia, near Turkey. (See also on p. 31.)

Gray Heron

|| *Ardea cinerea* ||
Class: Bird

Gray herons feed on freshwater fish and small mammals like shrews and field mice. They swallow fish whole, bones included, but often spit out any animal hair in the form of a pellet. They can also be found in Africa. (See also on p. 55.)

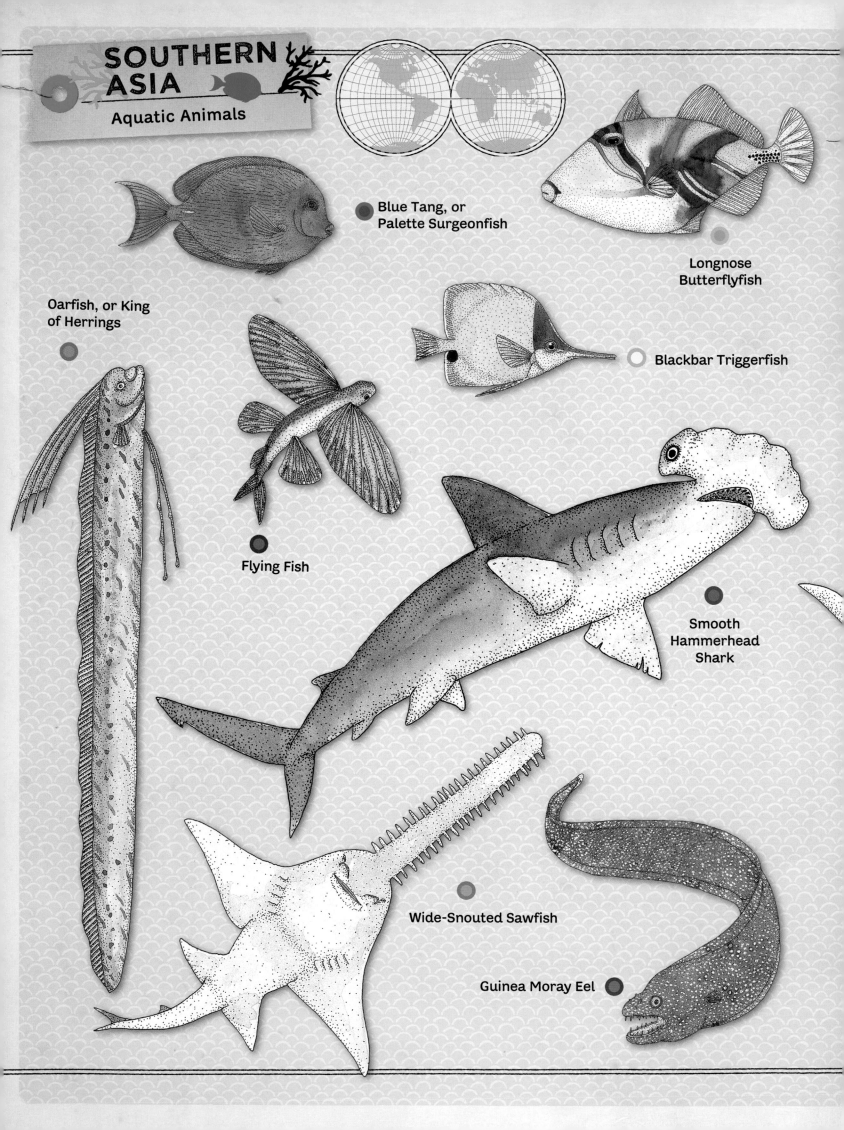

SOUTHERN ASIA
Aquatic Animals

Blue Tang, or Palette Surgeonfish

Longnose Butterflyfish

Oarfish, or King of Herrings

Blackbar Triggerfish

Flying Fish

Smooth Hammerhead Shark

Wide-Snouted Sawfish

Guinea Moray Eel

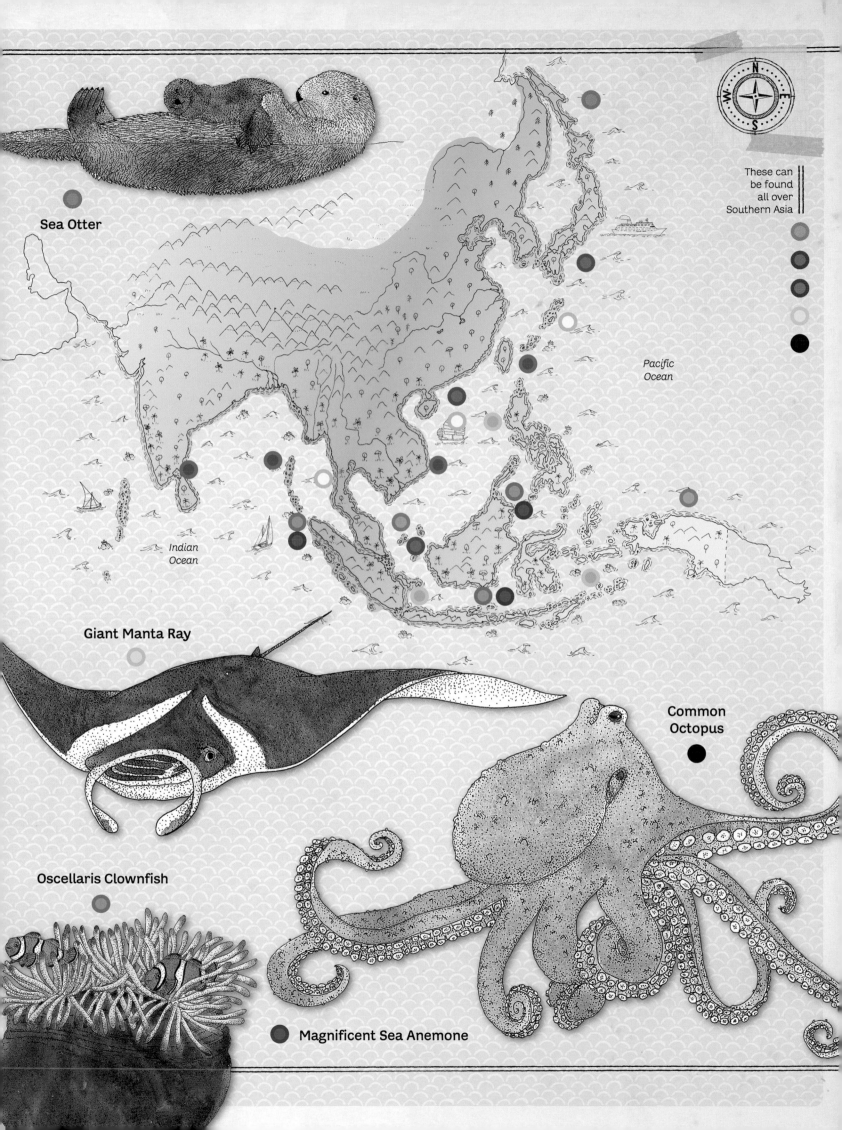

Sea Otter

These can
be found
all over
Southern Asia

*Pacific
Ocean*

*Indian
Ocean*

Giant Manta Ray

**Common
Octopus**

Oscellaris Clownfish

Magnificent Sea Anemone

SOUTHERN ASIA

Aquatic Animals

Oscellaris Clownfish
|| *Amphiprion ocellaris* ||
Class: Bony fish

Clownfish are able to live in venomous sea anemones because their bodies have a layer of mucus that protects them from the anemone's stinging cells.

Magnificent Sea Anemone
|| *Heteractis magnifica* ||
Class: Anthozoan

The magnificent sea anemone serves as home to numerous clownfish species, protecting them from predators while also feeding on the fish's scraps of food.

Guinea Moray Eel
|| *Gymnothorax meleagris* ||
Class: Bony fish

In its lagoon reef habitat, the Guinea moray spends its time hiding in holes or blending in with the rocky bottom. Their bodies can measure over 3 feet long.

Common Octopus
|| *Octopus vulgaris* ||
Class: Cephalopod

Found near the coast, octopuses are solitary except for reproduction. When the females lay eggs, they care for their eggs and rarely feed themselves, often dying soon after the hatching. An octopus can move by slithering at a slow crawl or by propelling itself by squirting jets of water. Humans fish octopuses for consumption. Octopuses are especially common in the coastal waters of Japan. (See also on p. 59 and p. 71.)

Oarfish, or King of Herrings
|| *Regalecus glesne* ||
Class: Bony fish

As its Latin name suggests, the oarfish is the "king of herrings." Its red dorsal fin starts at the top of its head with long rays forming a distinctive red crest. It also has two pelvic (or ventral) fins, which are long and thin. The giant oarfish will sometimes swim in a vertical position. Its long body—the longest of the bony fishes, with a record length of 36 feet—likely gave rise to legends of sea serpents.

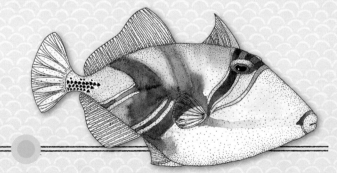

Blackbar Triggerfish
|| *Rhinecanthus aculeatus* ||
Class: Bony fish

This triggerfish, with a body up to 30 cm long, lives in the sandy areas of Pacific coral reefs. The blackbar triggerfish will aggressively defend its territory from intruders...including human divers. The blackbar and other triggerfish can also be found in Australia. (See also on p. 83.)

Longnose Butterflyfish

|| *Forcipiger longirostris* ||
|| Class: Bony fish ||

Using its long snout, which inspired its name, the longnose butterflyfish will pluck its hidden prey (often crustaceans) from crevices in the coral reef that other fish can't reach. Longnose butterflyfish have a yellow body with a black triangle on the head. They can be as long as 22 cm.

Flying Fish

|| *Exocoetus volitans* ||
|| Class: Bony fish ||

Despite its common name, the flying fish doesn't really fly; it jumps and then glides long distances, sometimes for over 650 feet and 4 feet above the water's surface. Its four pectoral fins are highly developed and act almost like sails.
(See also on p. 70.)

Wide-Snouted Sawfish

|| *Pristis microdon* ||
|| Class: Cartilaginous fish ||

The wide-snouted sawfish's rostrum, or "saw," is a rigid bill covered on both sides by a line of 14 to 22 teeth. This distinctive feature is used for digging in the ground to find food. It also has wide nostrils with nasal openings and high, pointed dorsal fins.
(See also on p. 58.)

Blue Tang, or Palette Surgeonfish

|| *Paracanthurus hepatus* ||
|| Class: Bony fish ||

The juvenile surgeonfish is yellow, while the adult is an intense blue. Spikes located around the tail fin prick up when the fish is threatened, earning its name the "surgeonfish." Algae is its only food source, though. Its well-formed mouth looks like a human mouth.

Smooth Hammerhead Shark

|| *Sphyrna zygaena* ||
|| Class: Cartilaginous fish ||

Extensions on both sides of this shark's head give it the hammer shape; its eyes are located on both ends of the hammer. These sharks feed on fish and crustaceans in the Indian Ocean, as well as in the temperate waters of the Atlantic and the Mediterranean. (See also on p. 11.)

Sea Otter

|| *Enhydra lutris* ||
|| Class: Mammal ||

Sea otters are the only otters that can spend months in the water without returning to land. They are kept warm by their thick fur, not by layers of fat like many other animals. (See also on p. 35.)

Giant Manta Ray

|| *Manta birostris* ||
|| Class: Cartilaginous fish ||

The largest ray in the world, the giant manta ray has highly developed pectoral fins based near its head and tail. The mouth is located on its ventral side and it often rests on the seafloor to eat while breathing through small openings on its dorsal side.

AFRICA
Land Animals

Common
Chimpanzee

Leopard

Black Rhinoceros

Flap-Necked Chameleon

Ostrich

Fennec
Fox

Plains Zebra

Arabian Camel

Meerkat

Western
Gorilla

Lion and Lioness

Ring-Tailed Lemur

Giraffe

Springbok

African Bush Elephant

AFRICA

Land Animals

Black Rhinoceros
|| *Diceros bicornis* ||
Class: Mammal

Despite its name, this large mammal is gray in color and can easily be recognized by the two horns on its head. Black rhinos live in the tropical forest or the savanna, where they wallow in the mud to ward off parasites and keep cool. They have thick skin but are nearly hairless.

Flap-Necked Chameleon
|| *Chamaeleo dilepis* ||
Class: Reptile

This large chameleon can reach lengths of 30 cm. Found on branches in the tropical forest, it waits and watches for its prey with eyes that move independently of each other. Its tongue reaches out suddenly, sticking to the insect, butterfly, or grasshopper. This particular chameleon species has neck flaps behind its head that expand whenever threatened.

Leopard
|| *Panthera pardus* ||
Class: Mammal

This feline uses its muscular forelegs to jump up on a branch in order to rest or eat its prey. The leopard's fur serves as camouflage among the grass and trees of its habitat in the forest, mountains, or steppes. (See also on p. 38.)

Lion and Lioness
|| *Panthera leo* ||
Class: Mammal

The lion, a majestic feline with a large mane, lives in groups roaming the savanna; lions defend the territory of their pride, or family. The lioness is a fast and fierce hunter of wildebeest, antelope, and zebra.

Fennec Fox
|| *Vulpes zerda* ||
Class: Mammal

The "desert fox," a small carnivore with long legs and sharp teeth, hunts at night for rodents, birds, lizards, and insects. During the day, its long ears help the fennec regulate its temperature in the scorching desert by spreading its body heat.

Ring-Tailed Lemur
|| *Lemur catta* ||
Class: Mammal

This little lemur, an endangered primate, is endemic to southern Madagascar. It is known for sunbathing in the morning way up high in the trees of the island's savanna. When on the ground, it walks around with its black-and-white striped tail raised. During mating season, the ring-tailed lemur releases an unpleasant odor that initiates stink fights between males.

Western Gorilla
|| *Gorilla gorilla* ||
Class: Mammal

This great ape primarily lives on the ground in the tropical forest, feeding on leaves, fruits, and roots. Its long hair protects it from the high mountains' cold temperatures. Male gorillas will beat their chest to scare off enemies. They sleep on the ground while the females and their young make a nest in the trees. The mother remains faithful to her mate.

Arabian Camel
|| *Camelus dromedarius* ||
|| Class: Mammal ||

This hardy mammal is herbivorous—it especially likes eating the leaves of acacia trees—and an excellent runner. The camel is adapted to life in the desert: long hairs protect its eyes and ears, its nostrils close up in case of a sandstorm, and it can go several days without drinking. Rather than hooves, the camel has toes padded with soft tissue for walking on sand.

Ostrich
|| *Struthio camelus* ||
|| Class: Bird ||

The ostrich is not only the largest bird in the world but also the fastest, running at speeds up to 43 miles per hour; however, it cannot fly. This long-necked bird with strong legs and two toes on each foot can be found living in sandy regions, savannas, or open woodlands. They feed on seeds, fruits, and little mammals. The male can be 9 feet tall. The female has gray feathers and lays the largest eggs in the world, sometimes weighing over 3 lbs.

Plains Zebra
|| *Equus quagga* ||
|| Class: Mammal ||

Zebras can be found grazing in herds in the savanna not far from a water source. They have long narrow heads, large ears, and stripes. If in danger, zebras can run extremely fast. They are only found in Africa.

African Bush Elephant
|| *Loxodonta africana* ||
|| Class: Mammal ||

The African bush elephant is the biggest animal on earth, standing 13 feet tall and weighing up to 9 tons. They live in the savanna or in swampy areas where, despite their size, they're agile and can swim. Males are solitary while females live in herds with their young. Elephants use their nimble trunks to eat fruit, bark, and leaves.

Meerkat
|| *Suricata suricatta* ||
|| Class: Mammal ||

This little carnivore found in the Namib desert lives in colonies of three to twenty-five individuals. When meerkats leave their burrow, one or two always remain behind as lookouts to warn the others with their bark-like cries in case of danger. They use their claws to dig through the sand for prey and have transparent eyelids that lower to protect their eyes from sand. They're extreme insectivores and can even eat poisonous scorpions.

Springbok
|| *Antidorcas marsupialis* ||
|| Class: Mammal ||

This savanna antelope leaps in the air—jumping as high as 10 feet thanks to its long, thin legs. They may leap to flee from predators, like the lion.

Giraffe
|| *Giraffa camelopardalis* ||
|| Class: Mammal ||

The giraffe is the tallest land animal: males can reach 18 feet tall, and females 15 feet tall. Thanks to their long necks, giraffes eat the acacia leaves that other herbivores can't reach. They can run almost as fast as a lion, with a type of movement called ambling, meaning the left legs move together followed by the right, like the dromedary.

Common Chimpanzee
|| *Pan troglodytes* ||
|| Class: Mammal ||

This primate belongs to the great ape family, which is genetically closely related to humans. They live in troops in the tropical forest, often hanging from the trees by their long, flexible arms. When on the ground, they move around on all fours. They're omnivorous, feeding mainly on fruit, leaves, flowers, seeds, and insects, but they also feed on small monkeys. The chimpanzee is known for its numerous calls and its ability to mimic.

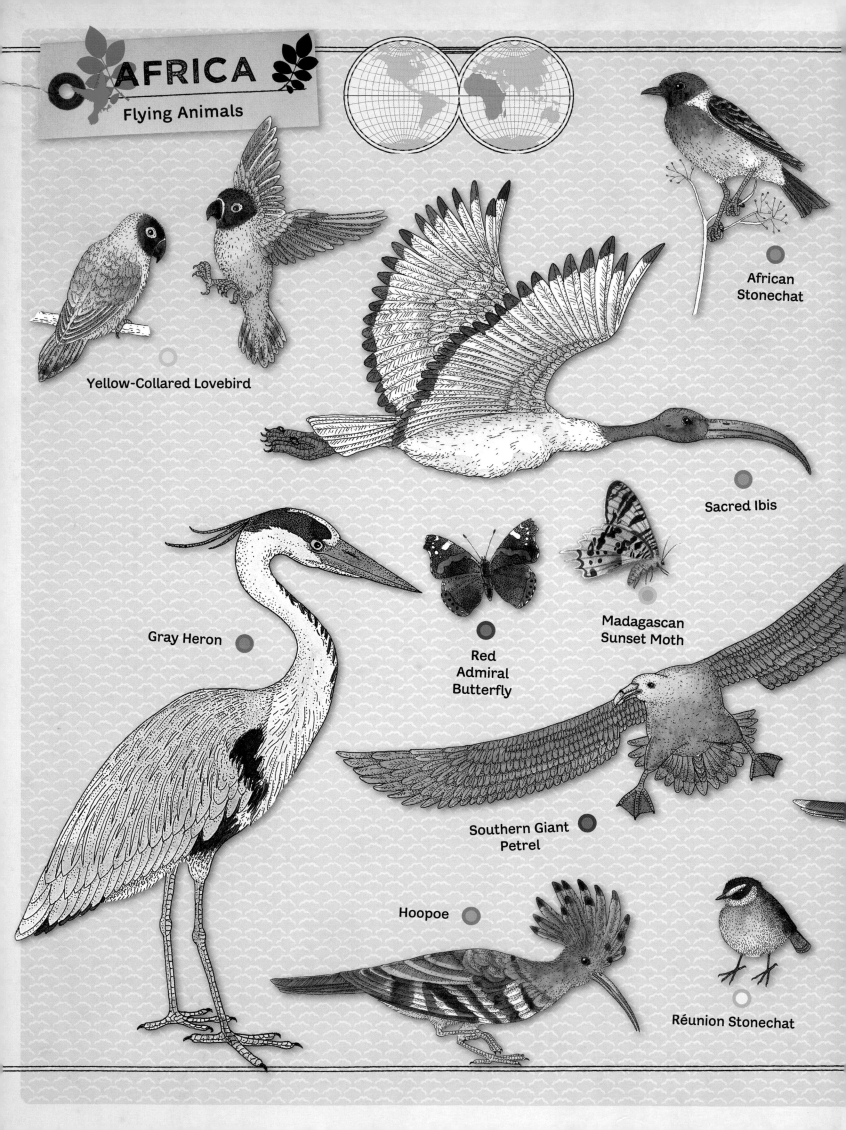

AFRICA

Flying Animals

African Stonechat

Yellow-Collared Lovebird

Sacred Ibis

Gray Heron

Red Admiral Butterfly

Madagascan Sunset Moth

Southern Giant Petrel

Hoopoe

Réunion Stonechat

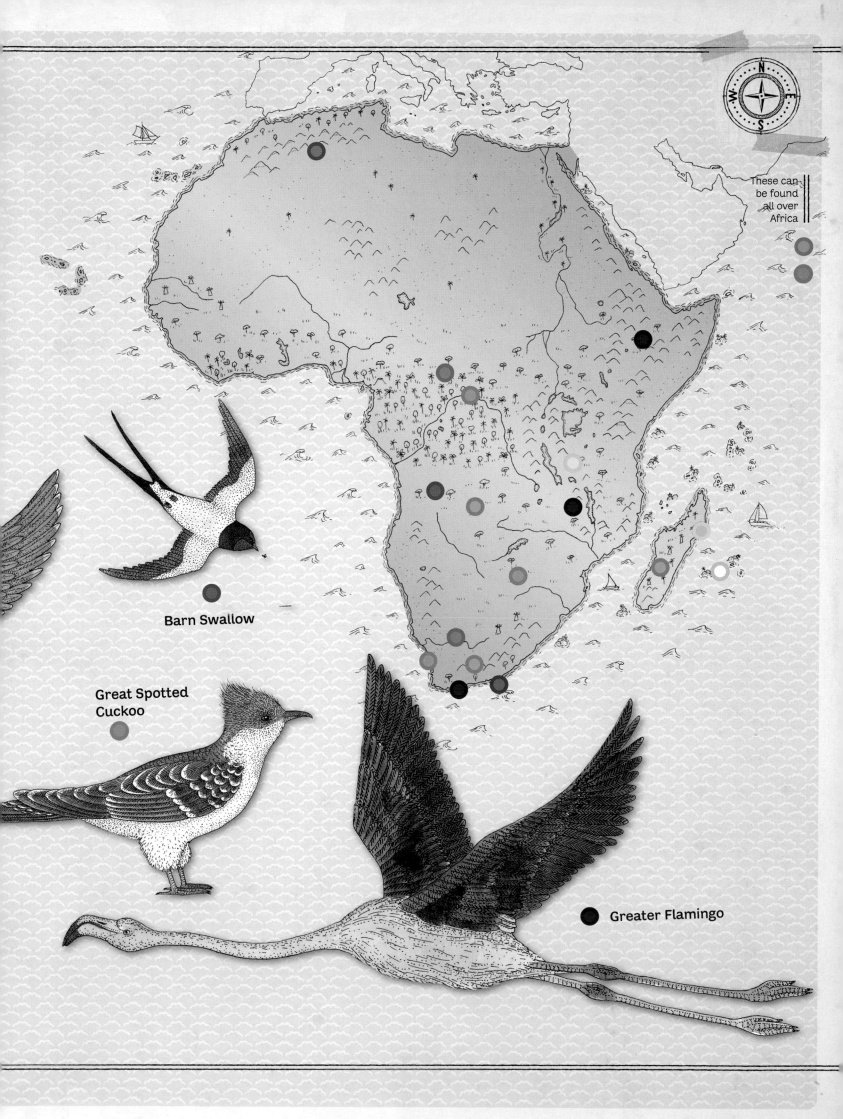

These can
be found
all over
Africa

Barn Swallow

**Great Spotted
Cuckoo**

Greater Flamingo

AFRICA

Flying Animals

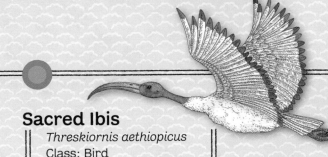

Sacred Ibis
|| *Threskiornis aethiopicus*
|| Class: Bird
The black-and-white ibis, with its bare neck, was sacred to the ancient Egyptians. The ibis live in sub-Saharan Africa near humans, feeding on garbage, animal carcasses, freshwater animals, and insects. They were accidentally introduced in Brittany after wandering away from a zoo. Its cousin, the scarlet ibis, can be found in Central and South America.

Hoopoe
|| *Upupa africana*
|| Class: Bird
The hoopoe's black and rust striped crest can be flattened backward or raised upright like a crown when it feels threatened. The hoopoe uses its long, thin, curved beak to find insects in the ground. It will then smack its prey against the ground to remove its wings and feet, tossing it into the air afterward and opening its beak wide! They also eat small frogs.

Greater Flamingo
|| *Phoenicopterus roseus*
|| Class: Bird
The greater flamingo—the largest of the flamingos—is a type of wading bird with a long neck that lives in flocks of thousands in freshwater or saltwater. To eat, the flamingo plunges its head underwater and uses its downward-curved bill to filter microorganisms (tiny plants and animals). The male and female take turns incubating their single egg, which then joins with the other hatchlings after birth.

African Stonechat
|| *Saxicola torquatus*
|| Class: Bird
The male African stonechat can be identified by its black head and red upper breast. Solitary or mated, these birds spend their time in the undergrowth or perched on branches, waiting for flying or crawling insects. The African stonechat is a little "plump," due to its mostly sedentary life.

Yellow-Collared Lovebird
|| *Agapornis personatus*
|| Class: Bird
This parrot has a white circle around its eyes and lives with its mate; the male and female preen, or groom, each other's feathers. Like all parrots, lovebirds can climb; in addition to using their feet, they also use their bright red beak as a third limb. The lovebird's beak has independent jawbones that make it incredibly flexible. The lower mandible is used for crushing up fruit, nutshells, and seeds.

Red Admiral Butterfly

|| *Vanessa atalanta* ||
Class: Insect

This migratory butterfly has orange bands on a black background and can be found in the temperate northern hemisphere. It feeds on flower nectar and fruit juice, such as apples that have fallen to the ground. (See also on p. 6.)

Madagascan Sunset Moth

|| *Chrysiridia rhipheus* ||
Class: Insect

The Madagascan sunset moth is a large day-flying moth found only in Madagascar. Its wings are black and green with golden spots and have several light-blue or white "tails." These moths migrate between the forests on the east and west coasts of the island, living on vines.

Gray Heron

|| *Ardea cinerea* ||
Class: Bird

Mostly solitary, this large wading bird makes its nest in tall trees near ponds and wades in the shallow water, catching fish, frogs, and other aquatic animals. When in flight, the gray heron's S-shaped neck sets it apart from cranes and swans. (See also on p. 43.)

Réunion Stonechat

|| *Saxicola tectes* ||
Class: Bird

Endemic to Réunion Island, this little bird with white eyebrows lives in forest clearings. They live alone and hunt for insects while in flight or on the ground. They nest in the hollow of trees or on the ground.

Great Spotted Cuckoo

|| *Clamator glandarius* ||
Class: Bird

The great spotted cuckoo has a light underbelly, contrasting with the dark brown or black color of its back, wings, and tail, which include white spots. The adult has a gray crest. This migratory bird spends the winter in sub-Saharan Africa. (See also on p. 18.)

Barn Swallow

|| *Hirundo rustica* ||
Class: Bird

The barn swallow lives in a variety of areas and feeds in open areas such as fields, parks, and the sides of roads. They build nests under the eaves or the inside of sheds, barns, bridges and other structures. This migratory bird can be found in northern Asia as well. (See also on p. 18 and p. 30.)

Southern Giant Petrel

|| *Macronectes giganteus* ||
Class: Bird

This giant petrel only lives in the southern hemisphere, primarily on islands or Antarctica. They have been found as far as the Gough Island, in the southern Atlantic, 1,700 miles from the cape of Africa. Seal and penguin carcasses are these birds main source of food, though they also feed on fish discarded from ships. (See also on p. 90.)

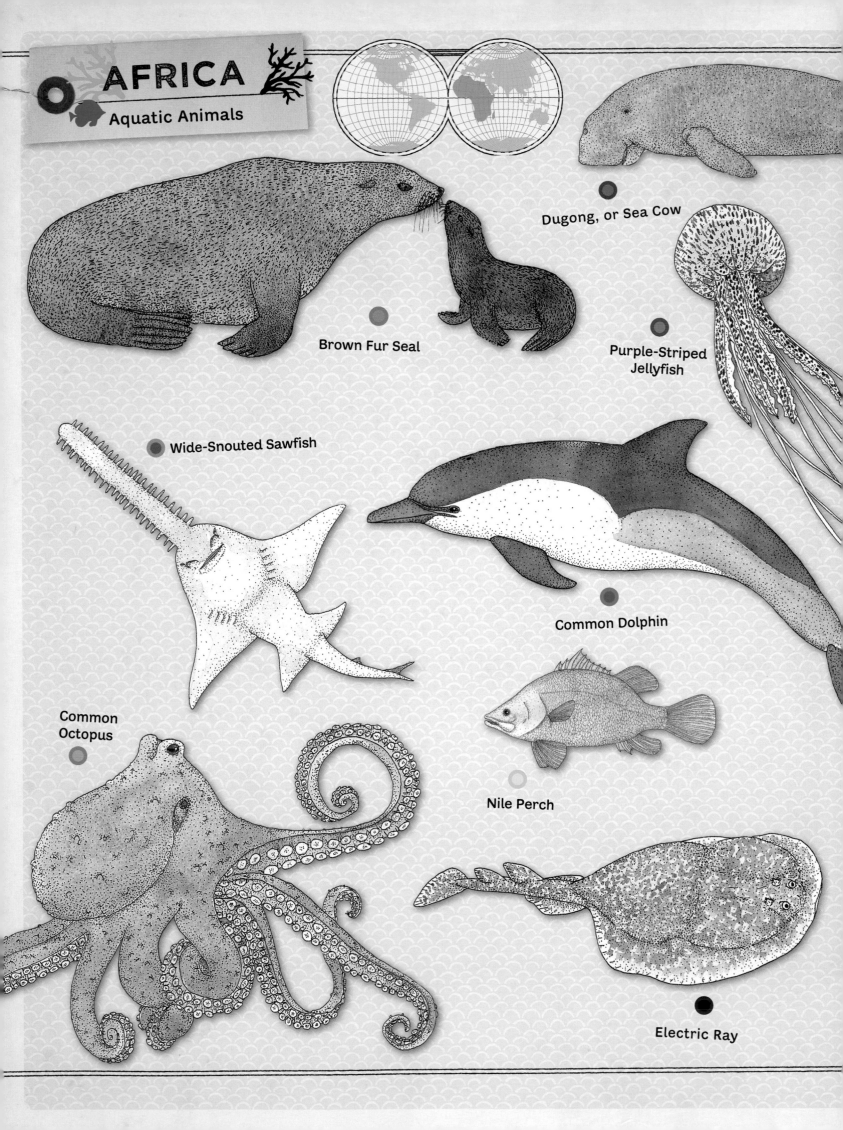

AFRICA
Aquatic Animals

Dugong, or Sea Cow

Brown Fur Seal

Purple-Striped Jellyfish

Wide-Snouted Sawfish

Common Dolphin

Common Octopus

Nile Perch

Electric Ray

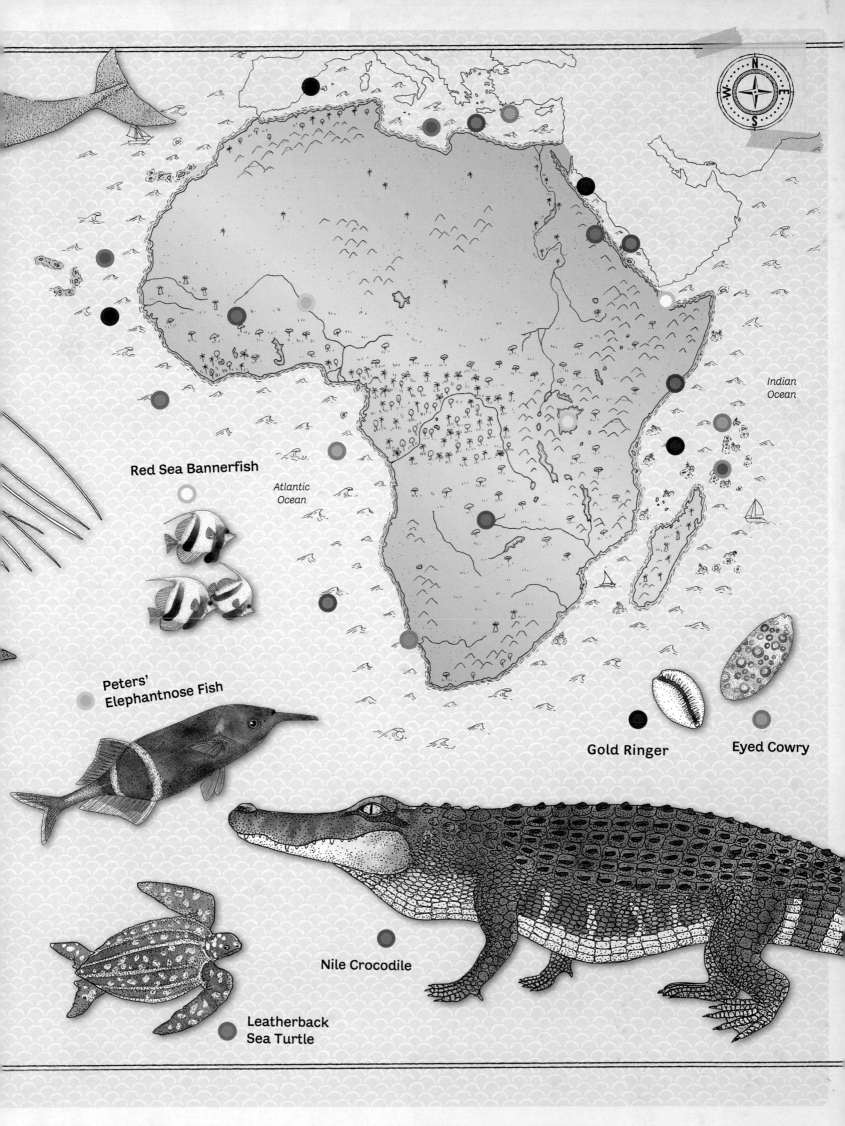

Red Sea Bannerfish

Atlantic
Ocean

Indian
Ocean

Peters'
Elephantnose Fish

Gold Ringer

Eyed Cowry

Nile Crocodile

Leatherback
Sea Turtle

AFRICA

Aquatic Animals

Nile Perch

|| *Lates niloticus*
|| Class: Bony fish ||

This ferocious freshwater predator, some-times confused with the family of fish called "emperors," is native to the Nile. Nile perch can weigh up to 440 lbs. and measure 6.5 feet long. They are a popular source of food and have been introduced throughout Africa.

Peters' Elephantnose Fish

|| *Gnathonemus petersii* ||
|| Class: Bony fish ||

This freshwater fish found in west and central Africa is especially prominent in the Niger River. It has a sensitive snout—an extension of its chin—used for self-defense, communication, and finding worms or insects in the sand. Their food hunting takes place at night.

Dugong, or Sea Cow

|| *Dugong dugon*
|| Class: Mammal ||

One of the most critically endangered species, dugongs can be found grazing on seagrasses in the shallow coastal waters of the Indian Ocean. Dugongs are the only entirely marine mammal to have an exclusive plant diet. A wide muzzle conceals the dugong's best weapon: two tusks. (See also on p. 96.)

Nile Crocodile

|| *Crocodylus niloticus* ||
|| Class: Reptile ||

Despite its name, this large crocodile no longer lives in the Egyptian Nile, but in rivers and lakes all over Africa's tropics, especially in the south. The Nile crocodile, along with the saltwater crocodile, is the largest crocodile in the world: measuring up to 20 feet long. This crocodile has a long, pointed snout, webbed hind feet, and a tail that acts a pro-peller to move it forward in the water. They can also run as fast as 8.5 miles per hour.

Wide-Snouted Sawfish

|| *Pristis microdon* ||
|| Class: Cartilaginous fish ||

Sawfish are born in freshwater, then move to the ocean after several months. Their snouts, covered with a line of teeth, can be used to dig through the ground to find food. Wide-snouted sawfish are an endangered species, often getting tangled up in nets (or trawls), and for that reason no longer exist in the Mediterranean. (See also on p. 47.)

Brown Fur Seal

|| *Arctocephalus pusillus* ||
|| Class: Mammal ||

Brown fur seals, which live in colonies, are distin-guished from other seal species by their small ears and long neck. They are excellent swimmers, using their split hind flippers like a propeller, and primar-ily hunt for food in the water. However, they can also use their front flippers to climb up on the rocks where they can catch birds.

Common Dolphin

|| *Delphinus delphis* ||
Class: Mammal

Strong swimmers with smooth skin and a slender body, dolphins move even when they are asleep, constantly coming up to the surface for air. These mammals live in temperate coastal waters in groups, called pods, with up to 10,000 individuals.

Purple-Striped Jellyfish

|| *Pelagia noctiluca* ||
Class: Scyphozoa

Jellyfish move in groups of hundreds or thousands, which follow the flow of the ocean's current. Purple-striped jellyfish can be found in the Atlantic Ocean. Their four arms and eight stinging tentacles are constantly in motion. When disturbed, they eject a bioluminescent, or glowing, mucus. They also live in the Mediterranean and the Red Sea.

Common Octopus

|| *Octopus vulgaris* ||
Class: Cephalopod

The octopus moves rapidly by jet propulsion using its siphon. It can disappear unseen by projecting a cloud of black ink, and its skin can change color to camouflage with its surroundings. It uses its eight tentacles to grab mollusks and crustaceans as food, crushing them up with its beak. It can be found south of North America and in Asia. (See also on p. 46 and p. 71.)

Leatherback Sea Turtle

|| *Dermochelys coriacea* ||
Class: Reptile

Leatherback sea turtles are the largest of all living turtles. Their shell has seven ridges and their diet consists of jellyfish. These turtles migrate thousands of miles through various fairly temperate oceans. Females lay their eggs at night on sandy tropical beaches. (See also on p. 82.)

Electric Ray

|| *Torpedo nobiliana* ||
Class: Bony fish

Found on the ocean floor, the round, flat ray known as the electric ray covers and electrocutes its prey—using electric organs visibly located in its disc—before eating.

Red Sea Bannerfish

|| *Heniochus intermedius* ||
Class: Bony fish

This butterflyfish, measuring 18 cm in length, lives in the coral reef. They have very fine hairlike teeth that enable them to pick out small organisms inaccessible to most other fish for eating.

Eyed Cowry

|| *Cypraea argus* ||
Class: Gastropod

Living in eastern Africa, eyed cowries are a species of sea snail. The animal hides inside its thick shell.

Gold Ringer

|| *Monetaria annulus* ||
Class: Gastropod

Gold ringers, or ring cowries, live in the Red Sea and Indian Ocean where they attach to rocks or algae. They have a distinctive orange ring on top of their shell.

SOUTH AMERICA
Land Animals

Black-Headed
Spider Monkey

Dyeing Dart Frog

Brown-Throated
Sloth

Green Iguana

Maned Wolf

Strawberry
Poison Frog

Brazilian
Porcupine

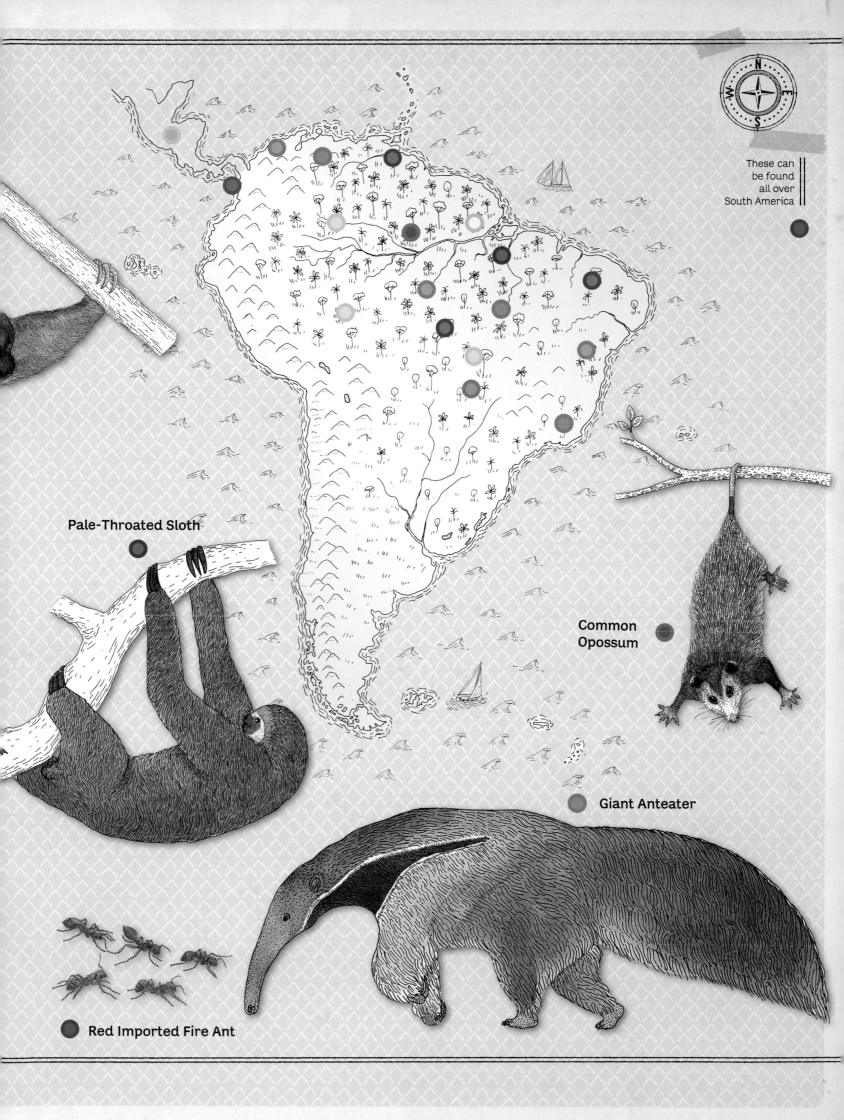

These can be found all over South America

Pale-Throated Sloth

Common Opossum

Giant Anteater

Red Imported Fire Ant

SOUTH AMERICA

Land Animals

Brazilian Porcupine

|| *Coendou prehensilis* ||
Class: Mammal

This tree-dwelling porcupine feeds on plants. Its body is covered with white-tipped quills, and it has a long tail it uses to dangle from tree branches.

Green Iguana

|| *Iguana iguana* ||
Class: Reptile

The green or gray color of this lizard allows it to blend in, despite the fact that its body can be almost 7 feet long. It has a row of spines along its back and a black-banded tail that it uses like a whip.

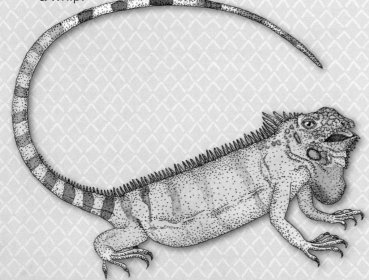

Black-Headed Spider Monkey

|| *Ateles fusciceps* ||
Class: Mammal

The black-headed spider monkey moves quickly among the trees using its legs and long tail, which acts like a fifth limb. They live in troops of twenty to thirty individuals feeding on the ripe fruit of the canopy. When danger is present, they bark.

Dyeing Dart Frog

|| *Dendrobates tinctorius* ||
Class: Amphibian

Often living in trees, this little frog's brightly colored skin warns predators of its poison. In the past, Amazonian Indians cooked the dyeing dart frog to gather its toxic venom, which they would then smear on the tips of their arrows. Dyeing dart frogs are part of the family known as poison dart frogs.

Maned Wolf

|| *Chrysocyon brachyurus* ||
Class: Mammal

The maned wolf lives in tallgrass prairies. The adult has a red coat and black mane, while the black portion of its long legs looks as if it's wearing socks.

Common Opossum

|| *Didelphis marsupialis* ||
Class: Mammal

This opossum sleeps during the day and is active at night. Its eyes are adjusted to the darkness. When threatened, it releases a foul odor to ward off predators or plays dead. (See also on p. 3.)

Brown-Throated Sloth

|| *Bradypus variegatus* ||
Class: Mammal

Brown-throated sloths—the most common sloth species—hang from trees or sit on branches, living a quiet, rather lazy lifestyle. Their diet mainly consists of leaves. Their features include a blunt nose and short tail, and their main activity consists of sleeping a dozen hours each day.

Pale-Throated Sloth

|| *Bradypus tridactylus* ||
Class: Mammal

This three-toed sloth moves slowly around the tree canopy of its habitat, the tropical rainforest, and is known for sleeping twenty hours per day. Algae grow on its hair and turn the sloth a greenish color, which intensifies as it ages.

Red Imported Fire Ant

|| *Solenopsis invicta* ||
Class: Insect

These ants eat plants, insects, and even fledglings who have not yet flown the nest. They can have a disastrous impact on plants and wildlife! Native to South America, they are also found in southern Asia and recently in the southern Pacific. (See also on p. 38 and p. 75.)

Giant Anteater

|| *Myrmecophaga tridactyla* ||
Class: Mammal

The giant anteater rips open anthills or termite mounds with its claws and then vacuums up the insects with the help of its long, sticky tongue.

Strawberry Poison Frog

|| *Oophaga pumilio* ||
Class: Amphibian

Found in Central America, this tiny little frog's vibrant coloring warns predators of its toxic skin. These toxins are also lethal for humans.

SOUTH AMERICA

Flying Animals

Channel-Billed Toucan

Scarlet Macaw

Pansy Daggerwing

Northern House Mosquito

Scarlet Ibis

Andean Condor

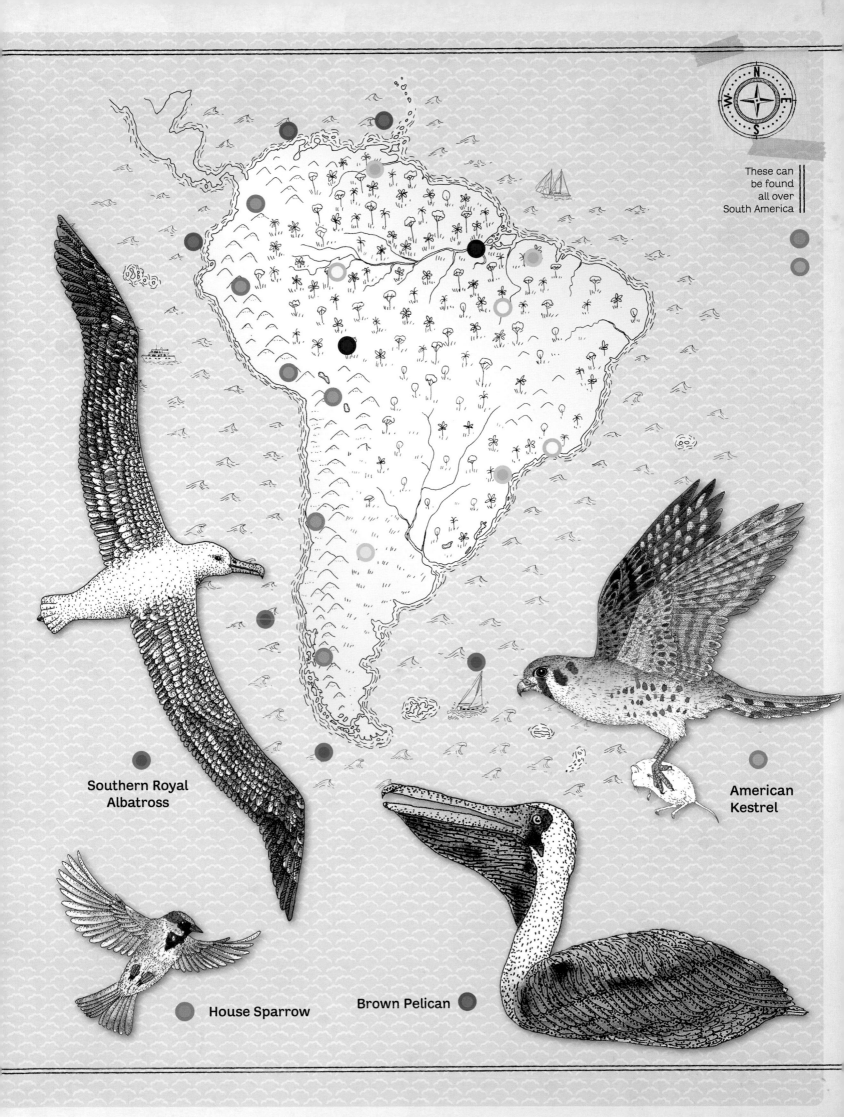

These can
be found
all over
South America

Southern Royal
Albatross

American
Kestrel

House Sparrow

Brown Pelican

SOUTH AMERICA

Flying Animals

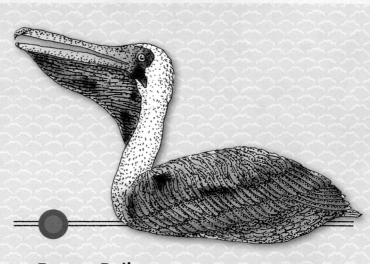

Brown Pelican
|| *Pelecanus occidentalis* ||
Class: Bird
Brown pelicans catch 4 lbs. of fish every day. They often feed on sardines and anchovies, using their expandable throat pouch like a net to scoop them up. They've been known to fight with other birds over food.

Southern Royal Albatross
|| *Diomedea epomophora* ||
Class: Bird
The largest of the marine birds with a wingspan 10 feet wide, southern royal albatross, like all albatross, live in the southern seas. They eat squid and fish and occasionally crustaceans. (See also on p. 79.)

Northern House Mosquito
|| *Culex pipiens* ||
Class: Insect
Like all dipterans, northern house mosquitoes have a single pair of wings that remain tucked in next to the body when not in flight. All mosquitoes have long antennae (the males' are feathery). (See also on p. 7.)

Scarlet Ibis
|| *Eudocimus ruber* ||
Class: Bird
A long, thin bill makes the scarlet ibis able to fish the estuaries of large rivers or saltwater mangroves. They primarily eat shrimp, which is the reason for their bright coloration. To protect themselves from predators, ibis often make their nests in the same tree. The male and female both sit on the eggs and take turns feeding their young.

American Kestrel
|| *Falco sparverius* ||
Class: Bird
The kestrel is a small diurnal falcon found all over the Americas. Kestrels nest in existing spaces, like rock crevices, tree cavities, or man-made structures. Sometimes they kick out woodpeckers or squirrels to take their spot! (See also on p. 6.)

Scarlet Macaw

|| *Ara macao* ||
Class: Bird

The scarlet macaw lives in the tropical forest, most often in groups of twenty or more individuals. On average, they live to be fifty years old. They have magnificently colored feathers, mostly red, with yellow and blue on their wings, and white skin around their eyes. Thanks to their powerful beaks, macaws can eat hard-shelled fruits and seeds. This big parrot's main predators are nocturnal raptors.

Pansy Daggerwing

|| *Marpesia marcella* ||
Class: Insect

The pansy daggerwing's rear wings come to a pointed tip—like a dagger. Endemic to South and Central America, these butterflies live in the tropical rainforest.

House Sparrow

|| *Passer domesticus* ||
Class: Bird

Everywhere that humans live, this bird lives as well! House sparrows were first introduced to America in the nineteenth century. They prefer urban or residential zones where they primarily forage for food on the ground and roost together. Twelve feathers make up the house sparrow's rectrix, or tailfeathers, which helps steer its flight.

Andean Condor

|| *Vultur gryphus* ||
Class: Bird

This massive condor's head and neck are bare, while the rest of its body is covered with white and slick black feathers. The male has a caruncle, or fleshy lump, on the crown of its head. As scavengers, condors use their beaks to tear apart the flesh of dead animals, such as llamas. The female only lays one egg every two years in a crevice on the ground.

Channel-Billed Toucan

|| *Ramphastos vitellinus* ||
Class: Bird

The channel-billed toucan has black feathers on its back, wings, and tail; a yellow chest surrounded by white and red feathers; and a red rump. They're not very good fliers and mostly perch in trees in lowland forests, not far from water. Toucans use their huge, lightweight beaks to gulp down eggs and small animals or pick up fruit from the ground. This species is endemic to South America.

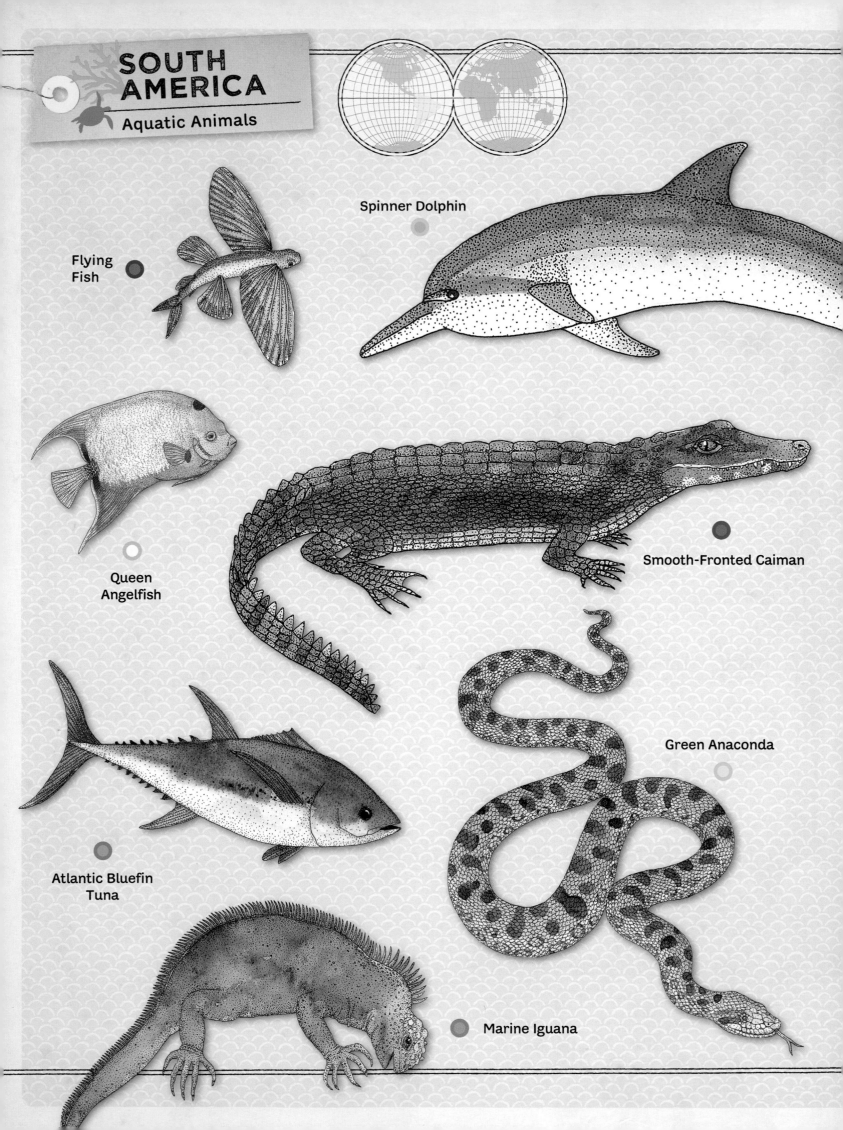

SOUTH AMERICA
Aquatic Animals

Spinner Dolphin

Flying Fish

Queen Angelfish

Smooth-Fronted Caiman

Green Anaconda

Atlantic Bluefin Tuna

Marine Iguana

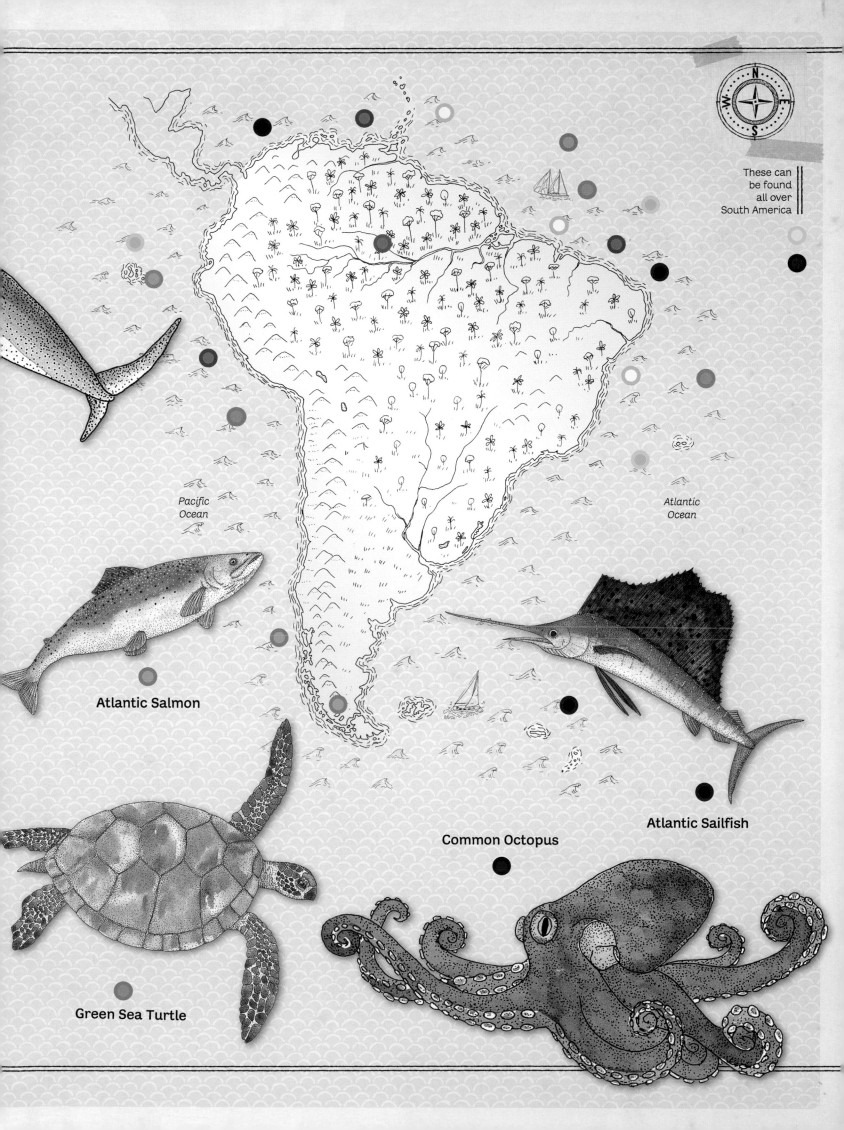

These can
be found
all over
South America

Pacific
Ocean

Atlantic
Ocean

Atlantic Salmon

Atlantic Sailfish

Common Octopus

Green Sea Turtle

SOUTH AMERICA

Aquatic Animals

Spinner Dolphin

|| *Stenella longirostris* ||
Class: Mammal

In tropical waters, this dolphin lives in groups, called pods, of 20 to 100 individuals. Spinner dolphins are known for their great acrobatic displays.

Smooth-Fronted Caiman

|| *Paleosuchus trigonatus* ||
Class: Reptile

Smooth-fronted caimans live in forested areas, hunting for small mammals. Caimans have shorter, wider snouts than their cousins, the crocodiles and gavials.

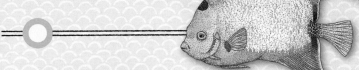

Flying Fish

|| *Exocoetus volitans* ||
Class: Bony fish

Flying fish inhabit the waters near the ocean's surface, feeding mainly on zooplankton. They fall prey to faster fish, like tuna or swordfish. More than 40 different flying fish species exist in the world. (See also on p. 47.)

Queen Angelfish

|| *Holacanthus ciliaris* ||
Class: Bony fish

Common in the West Indies, queen angelfish can also be found along the coast of Brazil. Living alone or with their mate, queen angelfish inhabit coral reefs where they find their preferred food source: sponges. They can reach up to 45 cm in length. (See also on p. 10.)

Atlantic Salmon

|| *Salmo salar* ||
Class: Bony fish

In the early twentieth century, Atlantic salmon were introduced in Argentina and Chile by the fishing industry. Salmon populations flourished best in the numerous lakes and rivers near the southern tip of Patagonia, so much so that they now form an exclusively freshwater subspecies. Chile produces more Atlantic salmon than any other country, besides Norway. (See also on p. 11.)

Atlantic Bluefin Tuna

|| *Thunnus thynnus* ||
Class: Bony fish

This large, warm-blooded fish (a rare characteristic for fish) lives off the coast of Venezuela and the Guiana Shield. They lay their eggs in the rough waters of the Gulf of Mexico then migrate to find food before returning to their mating ground. (See also on p. 11.)

Atlantic Sailfish

|| *Istiophorus albicans* ||
Class: Bony fish

Recognized by its extremely pointy jaw and distinctive dorsal fin that resembles a sail, Atlantic sailfish can be seen jumping out of the water. These large blue fish especially like the warm waters of the Atlantic. (See also on p. 11.)

Common Octopus

|| *Octopus vulgaris* ||
Class: Cephalopod

The common octopus, with its eight suction-padded tentacles, is extremely intelligent; octopuses have existed for millions of years. To escape danger, an octopus projects a cloud of black ink. This large mollusk lives in southern Asia and Africa as well. (See also on p. 46 and p. 59.)

Marine Iguana

|| *Amblyrhynchus cristatus* ||
Class: Reptile

This species, unique to the Galápagos Islands, is the only lizard in the world to inhabit a marine environment. Their main food source is algae. On land, the marine iguana breathes through its nostrils, using its nasal glands to excrete excess salt.

Green Anaconda

|| *Eunectes murinus* ||
Class: Reptile

The green anaconda is the largest snake in the world, weighing as much as 550 lbs. Males are usually about 10 feet long, and females measure to about 20 feet long. Anacondas crawl through the mud or swim in swampy freshwaters, hunting for rodents, birds, or little caimans. They are constrictors: they use their body to suffocate their prey.

Green Sea Turtle

|| *Chelonia mydas* ||
Class: Chelonian

As with all sea turtles, the green sea turtle's upper shell is lighter than that of land turtles and its head and legs do not retract. Its front legs' flipper shape is useful for swimming. Unlike other sea turtles, green sea turtles are herbivores; this diet consisting of algae and seagrass is what causes the turtles' green coloration.

AUSTRALIA
Land Animals

European Rabbit

Wild Boar

Koala

Frilled Lizard

Tasmanian Devil

Donkey

Ewe

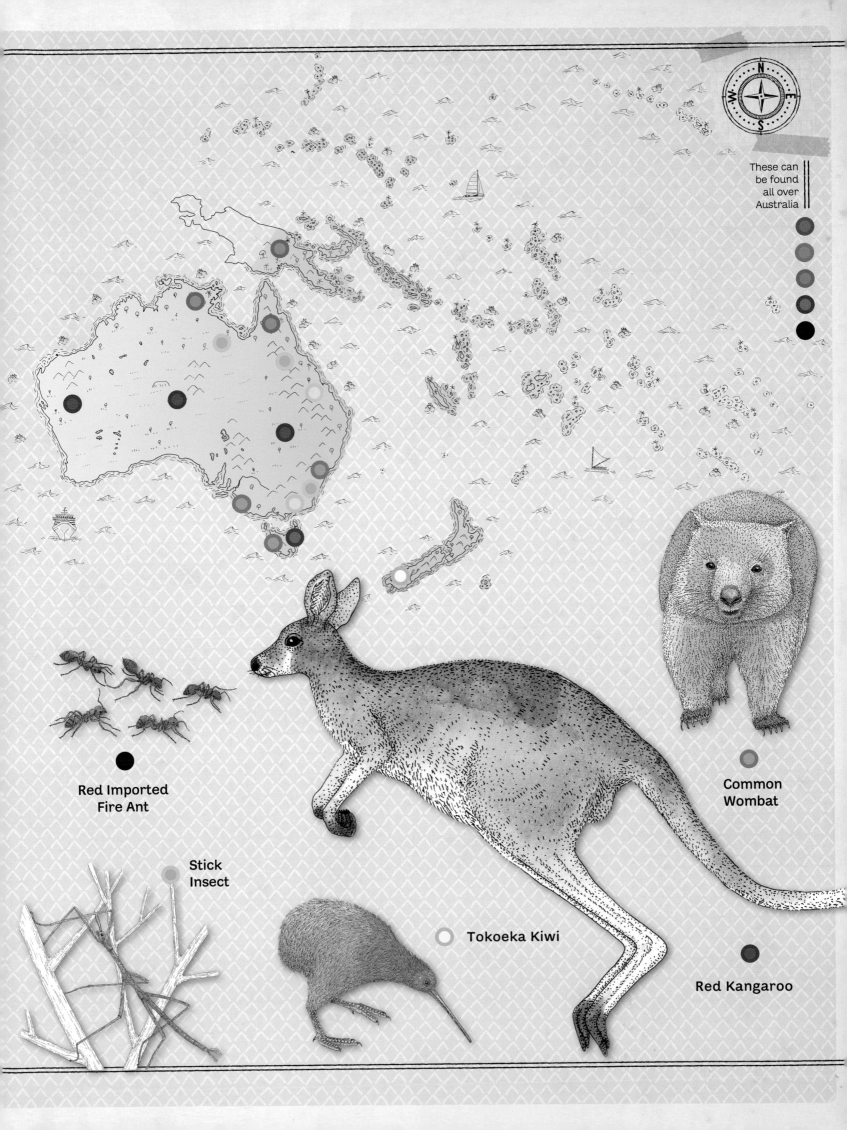

These can
be found
all over
Australia

Red Imported
Fire Ant

Stick
Insect

Tokoeka Kiwi

Common
Wombat

Red Kangaroo

AUSTRALIA

Land Animals

Tasmanian Devil

‖ *Sarcophilus harrisii* ‖
Class: Mammal

About the size of a dog, this black marsupial is the largest carnivore in Australia. More than 600 years ago, this species disappeared from the Australian mainland and now only lives on the island state of Tasmania. The name "devil" comes from its piercing cries. They hunt at night, and their teeth can gnaw through bone, like those of a wallaby. They also eat fish and birds.

Frilled Lizard

‖ *Chlamydosaurus kingii* ‖
Class: Reptile

This "Australian dragon" has an average length of 85 cm, but can be as long as 5 feet! Frilled lizards spend a great deal of time in the trees, feeding on insects. When faced with a predator, like a python or wildcat, the frilled lizard will stand on its back legs, spread out its frills (30 cm in diameter), and gape its mouth wide open.

Wild Boar

‖ *Sus scrofa* ‖
Class: Mammal

Wild boar can easily adapt to all types of plants once they find something to eat; in Australia, they inhabit the tropical rainforests or semidesert zones. While searching for food, wild boars destroy the ground beneath them, harming the local flora and fauna. (See also on p. 15 and p. 39.)

Ewe

‖ *Ovis aries* ‖
Class: Mammal

A ewe is a female sheep. Throughout the great plains of Australia, it is raised for its meat, milk, and semi-curly hair, called "wool."

European Rabbit

‖ *Oryctolagus cuniculus* ‖
Class: Mammal

Introduced by an Englishman in the nineteenth century, the European rabbit is now widespread in Australia. They live in colonies and dig numerous tunnels in the dry ground. The first rabbit to notice a threat will raise its white tail as a warning signal and tap the ground with its hind feet to alert the rest of the colony. (See also on p. 15.)

Donkey

‖ *Equus asinus* ‖
Class: Mammal

The main traits of the donkey are its large ears, long tail, and short stature. Donkeys were imported into Australia but then spread into the wild. This phenomenon is called "reintroduction."

Tokoeka Kiwi

Apteryx australis
Class: Bird

The tokoeka kiwi is one of five recognized species of kiwi. The name "kiwi" comes from a Maori word given to the bird: *kivi-kivi*. During evolution, this New Zealand bird's wings were reduced to mere stumps; it can no longer fly. The tokoeka kiwi lives with its mate. The kiwi's average lifespan is thirty to forty years.

Stick Insect

Ctenomorpha chronus
Class: Insect

Known as stick insects, this species has a remarkable ability to camouflage. The stick insect is the largest insect in the world, with a length reaching 30 cm. The stick insect is immobile during the day and moves about at night as it forages for food. It can self-amputate at will if a predator has caught one of its legs. Stick insects are especially common in tropical rainforests.

Common Wombat

Vombatus ursinus
Class: Mammal

This solitary, herbivorous marsupial is symbolic of Australia. Measuring an average of 3 feet tall, the wombat is the largest burrowing mammal, using its claws to dig tunnels. Active at night, the wombat moves about on all fours foraging for food. Female wombats have a marsupial pouch beneath the tail that opens toward the back, in which the embryo finishes developing. The wombat is a protected species in Australia.

Koala

Phascolarctos cinereus
Class: Mammal

A marsupial endemic to Australia, the koala has a large head and big fuzzy ears. The koala primarily feeds on eucalyptus leaves. Dense wooly fur near the koala's rump acts as a built-in "cushion." Koalas have been hunted for their fur for many years; the only ones remaining can be found on the eastern coast of Australia.

Red Imported Fire Ant

Solenopsis invicta
Class: Insect

These red ants native to South America were accidentally introduced into the southern Pacific region. They live in mounds, or piles of dirt, which are harmful to crops. If someone steps on their mound, the ants will come filing out in a swarm and attack the intruder! They can also be found in southern Asia. (See also on p. 38 and p. 63.)

Red Kangaroo

Macropus rufus
Class: Mammal

The largest of the kangaroos, the red kangaroo doesn't run, but rather hops around the arid plains of Australia. Its tail provides balance and acts as a springboard; red kangaroos can jump distances of up to 25 feet. When resting, red kangaroos stand upright using their hind legs and tail like a tripod.

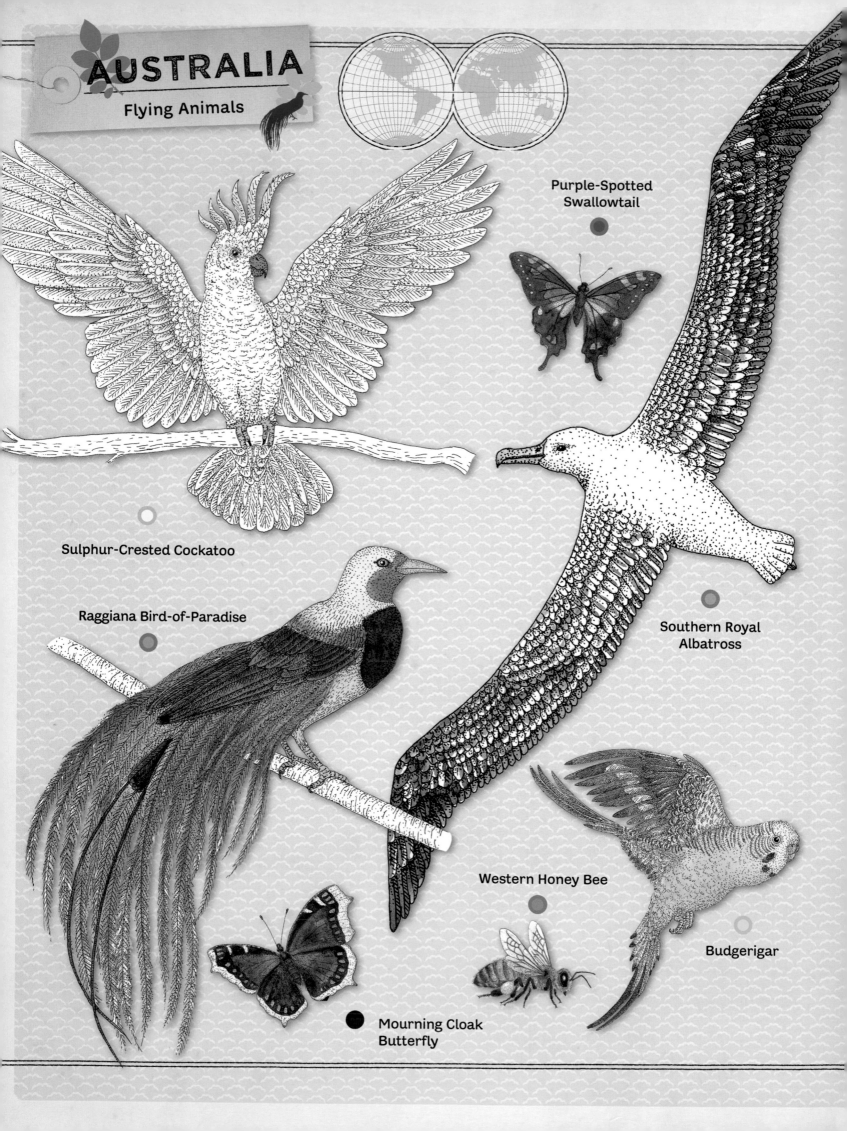

AUSTRALIA

Flying Animals

Purple-Spotted
Swallowtail

Sulphur-Crested Cockatoo

Raggiana Bird-of-Paradise

Southern Royal
Albatross

Western Honey Bee

Budgerigar

Mourning Cloak
Butterfly

These can be found all over Australia

Common Wasp

Mallard

Superb Fairy-Wren

Mute Swan

AUSTRALIA

Flying Animals

Sulphur-Crested Cockatoo
|| *Cacatua galerita* ||
Class: Bird

The sulphur-crested cockatoo is a large white parrot with a signature crest made up of 6 yellow feathers. These noisy birds are found only in certain parts of the south Pacific region. They fly at high altitudes then fall, or swoop, down in large, spiraling circles returning to the ground. As herbivores, cockatoos are detrimental to farms: they take seeds that have just been planted, eat ears of grain, and pierce the plastic hay bale coverings with their hooked beak.

Mourning Cloak Butterfly
|| *Nymphalis antiopa* ||
Class: Insect

A large daytime butterfly, the mourning cloak is known for its longevity; it can live up to 10 or 11 months. This butterfly is now rare. (See also on p. 42.)

Mute Swan
|| *Cygnus olor* ||
Class: Bird

Mute swans fly with their necks and heads held high, despite weighing 17 to 30 lbs., and can fly as fast as 53 mph. They can also swim. Due to their weight, they run on the water to gather speed before takeoff. (See also on p. 31.)

Mallard
|| *Anas platyrhynchos* ||
Class: Bird

The mallard is a dabbling duck, meaning it feeds in shallow water; it dips its head underwater and tips headfirst, raising its tail. Mallards also graze in the prairie. They are omnivorous; seeds, fish, grass, and insects are all included in their diet. (See also on p. 34.)

Superb Fairy-Wren
|| *Malurus cyaneus* ||
Class: Bird

The fairy-wren lives exclusively in the southern Pacific. During mating season, the male's coloring is brilliant blue while the female and non-reproducing male remain a darkish brown color. This noticeable difference is called "marked sexual dimorphism." The little fairy-wren has adapted to diverse habitats including pastures, gardens, and cities.

Southern Royal Albatross

|| *Diomedea epomophora* ||
Class: Bird

When fully extended, the southern royal albatross has a wingspan of about 10 feet, making it the largest marine bird in the world. Mates for life, the albatross meets with the same female once a year to reproduce. (See also on p. 66.)

Common Wasp

|| *Vespula vulgaris* ||
Class: Insect

The common wasp has a characteristic black abdomen with yellow stripes, as well as four wings (the two on each side act as one single wing) and a stinger. They are carnivorous insects that eat caterpillars and other garden pests. Unlike bees, wasps can sting several times without losing their stinger.

Budgerigar

|| *Melopsittacus undulatus* ||
Class: Bird

The budgerigar is an Australian nomadic bird with a melodious song. They flock in large groups in open spaces, like scrubland. The budgerigar's diet consists of grasses, spinifex seeds (a plant that grows in sandy areas), and occasionally grains. Its young are referred to as baby budgies. Budgerigars are the second most commonly domesticated birds in the world, after the canary.

Raggiana Bird-of-Paradise

|| *Paradisaea raggiana* ||
Class: Bird

Raggiana birds-of-paradise live in the tropical rain forests of Papua New Guinea where food is plentiful. The male has a yellow head, green neck, and light blue beak with a shimmering red tail during mating season. Male Raggiana birds-of-paradise are known for their lively mating dance, which involves a group of twenty other males and interruptions of many loud, nasal calls. This is how the females choose their mates.

Western Honey Bee

|| *Apis mellifera* ||
Class: Insect

Native to southeast Asia, western honey bees are now raised all over the world for their honey. In the summer, they feed by gathering nectar and pollen from flowers at the same time, which they then feed to their larvae. In the winter, they feed on the hive's honey. When threatened, they sting, but once a stinger has been broken, the bee will die soon after. (See also on p. 19.)

Purple-Spotted Swallowtail

|| *Graphium weiskei* ||
Class: Insect

The purple-spotted swallowtail is a nocturnal butterfly with purple spots that lives at an altitude between 5,000 and 8,000 feet.

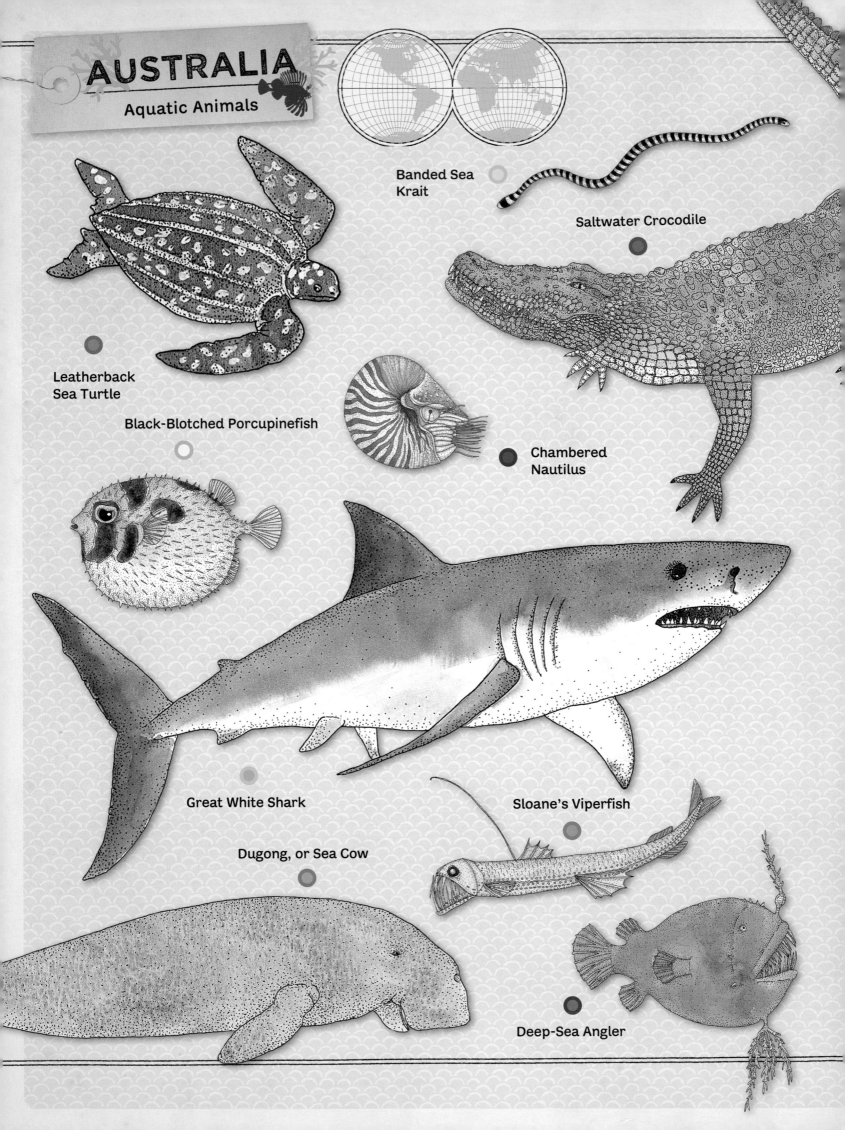

AUSTRALIA
Aquatic Animals

Banded Sea Krait

Saltwater Crocodile

Leatherback Sea Turtle

Black-Blotched Porcupinefish

Chambered Nautilus

Great White Shark

Sloane's Viperfish

Dugong, or Sea Cow

Deep-Sea Angler

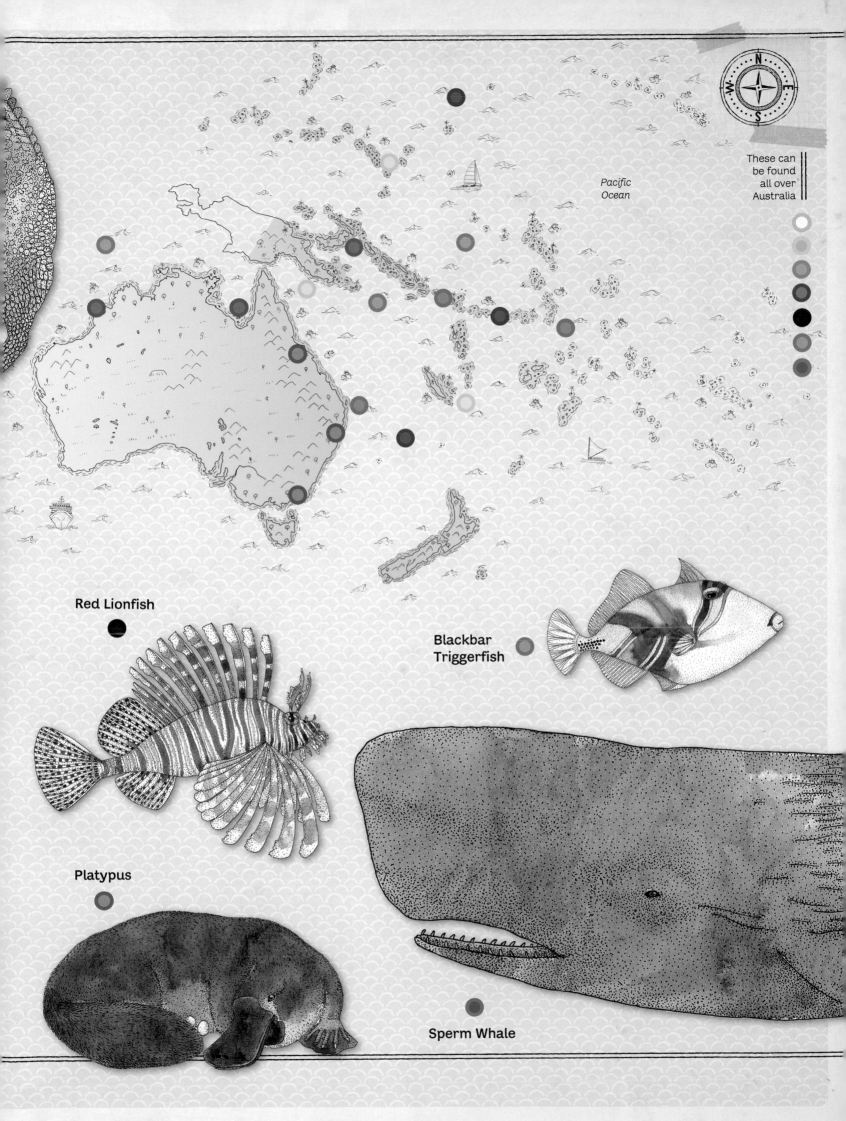

Pacific
Ocean

These can
be found
all over
Australia

Red Lionfish

Blackbar
Triggerfish

Platypus

Sperm Whale

AUSTRALIA

Aquatic Animals

Platypus
Ornithorhynchus anatinus
Class: Mammal
The platypus has a unique mouth that looks like a duckbill...and it is one of the only egg-laying mammals! Females can be found on the riverbanks of Australia keeping their eggs warm between their belly and tail, acting as a blanket. At birth, the mother nurses her young.

Leatherback Sea Turtle
Dermochelys coriacea
Class: Reptile
The leatherback sea turtle is the largest turtle in the world. Leatherback sea turtles also hold the record for long-distance swimming with a migration that can extend for several thousand miles! (See also on p. 59.)

Chambered Nautilus
Nautilus pompilius
Class: Cephalopod
Reaching about 8 inches long, this mollusk can be found off the coast of Australia, near the Pacific Islands and the Indian Ocean. This animal occupies the outermost chamber of its spiral-shaped shell. It has about ninety tentacles. The nautilus closely resembles its prehistoric ancestor, who lived 550 million years ago, well before the dinosaurs existed (200 million years ago).

Sperm Whale
Physeter macrocephalus
Class: Mammal
These large whales can be found in every ocean and sea, and they have the largest brains of any living mammal! Sperm whales feed on fish and squid, including giant squid (*Architeuthis dux*). (See also on p. 35 and p. 87.)

Sloane's Viperfish
Chauliodus sloani
Class: Bony fish
The viperfish's impressive jaw remains open, because long teeth prevent it from closing all the way! This fish lives in the abyss at up to 9,000 feet below sea level. (See also on p. 10.)

Dugong, or Sea Cow
Dugong dugon
Class: Mammal
The dugong's fluked tail sets it apart from a similar mammal, the manatee, which has a paddle-shaped tail. Its bark-like sound is called a "barbarouffement." Considered vulnerable to extinction, dugongs inhabit the shallow waters of the Pacific and Indian Oceans. (See also on p. 58.)

Deep-Sea Angler
Lophius piscatorius
Class: Bony fish
The deep-sea angler is one of four types of anglerfish that lives in the dark, cold zone of the ocean known as the abyss. A long multibranched barbel—which looks like a piece of algae—hanging from its lower jaw allows the anglerfish to "touch" things. The filament on its head is a bioluminescent organ that acts like a lure to attract prey.

Blackbar Triggerfish

|| *Rhinecanthus aculeatus*
|| Class: Bony fish

The blackbar triggerfish, also called a lagoon triggerfish, with its bright colorations and flattened body, has spikes on its back near the tail that keep predators at bay. When alarmed, the blackbar triggerfish makes audible noises. They can also be found in southern Asia. (See also on p. 46.)

Great White Shark

|| *Carcharodon carcharias*
|| Class: Cartilaginous fish

Great white sharks have knife-like triangular teeth used to rip apart their prey. When they lose a tooth, it's replaced by one from the next row (they have 4 to 6 rows of teeth). The great white shark is an excellent hunter due to its highly developed sense of smell, allowing it to smell a drop of blood from far away. (See also on p. 11.)

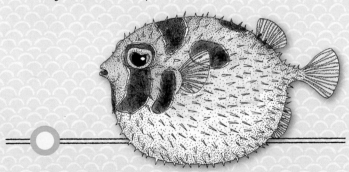

Black-Blotched Porcupinefish

|| *Diodon liturosus*
|| Class: Bony fish

This fish, living primarily in the coral reefs of Indonesia, has a unique trait of swallowing water and ballooning up when threatened. Under pressure, it raises its spines like a porcupine. The black-blotched porcupinefish has a poisonous pouch, making it toxic. Several different species of porcupinefish exist; this particular one has short spines.

Red Lionfish

|| *Pterois volitans*
|| Class: Bony fish

The red lionfish lives in coral reefs. Its pectoral fins look like wings and allow it to trap its prey in a corner before stunning the prey and eating it in one gulp. The red lionfish's dorsal spines are venomous, which protects it from predators.

Banded Sea Krait

|| *Laticauda colubrina*
|| Class: Reptile

This sea snake with a gray-blue body and black stripes is a fast swimmer, using its flat tail like a rudder. They often come to shore to lay their eggs. The banded sea krait is extremely venomous.

Saltwater Crocodile

|| *Crocodylus porosus*
|| Class: Reptile

This dangerous giant lives in mangroves and estuaries, particularly in Australia and Papua New Guinea, and can measure between 8 and 26 feet long. They swim long distances and lay their eggs in a nest on shore, keeping an eye on their eggs. The saltwater crocodile is hunted for its skin.

THE ARCTIC
Animals

Atlantic Puffin

Rock Ptarmigan

Killer Whale, or Orca

Common Sunstar

Krill

Blue Whale

Narwhal, or Unicorn Whale

Atlantic Mackerel

Sperm Whale

Walrus

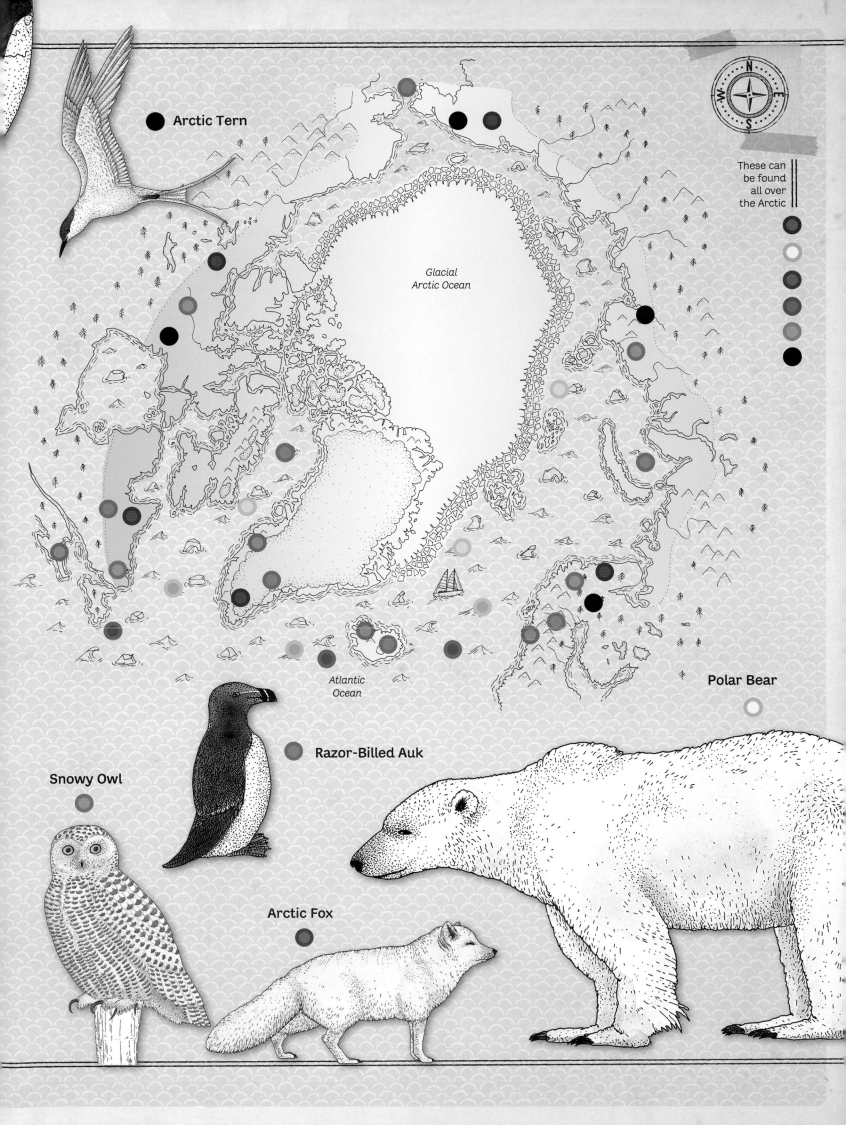

Arctic Tern

Glacial
Arctic Ocean

These can
be found
all over
the Arctic

Atlantic
Ocean

Polar Bear

Razor-Billed Auk

Snowy Owl

Arctic Fox

THE ARCTIC

Animals

Arctic Fox
|| *Alopex lagopus* ||
|| Class: Mammal ||

In the winter, the arctic fox has a very thick white coat, which blends in with the ice fields and protects it from the cold. In the summer, its fur is brown.

Atlantic Puffin
|| *Fratercula arctica* ||
|| Class: Bird ||

In Latin, the Atlantic puffin's scientific name means "the small brother of the Arctic," because its black-and-white feathers resemble a monk's habit. Puffins fish at depths of 50 to 200 feet and often swallow their prey immediately. They spend most of the year on the open ocean above the Arctic and Atlantic Oceans and return to the coast when it's time to reproduce. (See also on p. 18.)

Polar Bear
|| *Ursus maritimus* ||
|| Class: Mammal ||

This carnivorous bear is the ice field's giant, hiding its all-black skin beneath an all-white coat. They have slightly webbed feet that enable them to swim. They catch their main food source, seals, in their mouths.

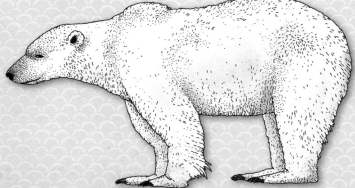

Rock Ptarmigan
|| *Lagopus muta* ||
|| Class: Bird ||

The rock ptarmigan can spend the entire year living above the Arctic Circle, unlike most other birds who migrate south in the winter. The males have a red wattle, or bit of flesh, above the eyes, which expands during mating season; females also have a wattle that is much less pronounced. (See also on p. 14.)

Arctic Tern
|| *Sterna paradisaea* ||
|| Class: Bird ||

The Arctic tern spends the summer in the Arctic Ocean, diving in to fish for food. In the winter, it migrates to Antarctica; the length of this migration causes the Arctic tern to spend eight months of the year in flight! Its extraordinary migration is one of its most important traits. (See also on p. 91.)

Krill
|| *Euphausia superba* ||
|| Class: Malacostracan ||

Along with many other species in their larval phase (crustaceans, fish, mollusks, etc.), these little cold-water crustaceans make up the zooplankton that serves as the primary food source for cetaceans (carnivorous, aquatic, marine mammals). Krill found in the Arctic differs from Antarctic krill: it includes different, more diverse species. (See also on p. 90.)

Blue Whale
|| *Balaenoptera musculus* ||
|| Class: Mammal ||

The blue whale, reaching 98 feet long, is the largest animal on the planet. It lives in deep water, but must return to the surface to breathe; like all mammals, blue whales have lungs! (See also on p. 91.)

Narwhal, or Unicorn Whale

Monodon monoceros
Class: Mammal

The narwhal swims slowly through the icy polar ocean due to its lack of dorsal fin. Narwhals live in groups. They're the most endangered Arctic species, even more so than the polar bear. (See also on p. 34.)

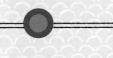

Common Sunstar

Crossaster papposus
Class: Asteroidia

This large starfish can have a diameter up to 35 cm wide. They generally have ten to twelve arms, which are covered with visible spines on top. They feed on other starfish, among other things.

Atlantic Mackerel

Scomber scombrus
Class: Bony fish

Juvenile Atlantic mackerel feed on plankton, filtering the water through their gills. They then move on to eating small fish in the summer and fall, but stop feeding in the winter when they move further south. (See also on p. 23.)

Killer Whale, or Orca

Orcinus orca
Class: Mammal

This hunter roams near beaches to attack penguins and sea lions. Out in the ocean, a group of killer whales may overtake a baby whale, separating it from its mother and drowning it by preventing it from resurfacing for air. They can also be found in Antarctica. (See also on p. 91.)

Razor-Billed Auk

Alca torda
Class: Bird

The razor-billed auk's short wings allow it to fly quickly and also serve as fins in the Arctic Ocean around Greenland; they arrive in Greenland in April and leave again in August to winter at sea. (See also on p. 7.)

Snowy Owl

Bubo scandiacus
Class: Bird

This large white owl can be 70 cm long, with the male generally slightly smaller than the female. Its yellow eyes, the same size as human eyes, are fixed, meaning it must turn its head in order to look around! Snowy owls primarily feed on lemmings. If food is scarce, they don't reproduce at all that year. Snowy owls can also be found in northern Asia. (See also on p. 30.)

Sperm Whale

Physeter macrocephalus
Class: Mammal

Only the male sperm whales adventure into the cold waters of Antarctica and the Arctic where they feed on fish and squid. These mammals feed primarily on octopus and squid, and some can live to be sixty years old. (See also on p. 35 and p. 82.)

Walrus

Odobenus rosmarus
Class: Mammal

Walruses live on ice fields in colonies of up to 8,000 individuals. In the water, the walrus's front flippers lay flat likes fins; on land, the front flippers are positioned forward, allowing the walrus to walk around. This carnivore can use its long tusks either as an ice pick or as a weapon when under attack! (See also on p. 34.)

ANTARCTICA
Animals

Southern Giant Petrel

Blue Whale

Imperial Shag

Arctic Tern

Killer Whale, or Orca

Emperor Penguin

Southern
Antarctic Ocean

These can
be found
all over
Antarctica

Crabeater Seal

Southern
Antarctic Ocean

**Humpback
Whale**

Krill

ANTARCTICA
Animals

Southern Giant Petrel
|| *Macronectes giganteus* ||
Class: Bird

This migratory bird, measuring up to 92 cm long, has a large beak used to pry open carcasses of seals or penguins on land. Other petrel species take to the air and feed far from the coasts. The southern giant petrel can also be found in Africa, depending on the season.
(See also on p. 55.)

Imperial Shag
|| *Phalacrocorax atriceps* ||
Class: Bird

The imperial shag is a large, swimming sea bird with blue rims around its eyes and webbing between the four toes on each foot. In the winter, imperial shags live as a group and feed out at sea. In the summer, they live and feed alone.

Crabeater Seal
|| *Lobodon carcinophaga* ||
Class: Mammal

This long, smooth seal is a fast swimmer, capable of reaching speeds of 16 miles per hour. Crabeater seals have teeth adapted to act as a filter, enabling them to feed on krill. They live exclusively in Antarctic and sub-Antarctic waters.

Krill
|| *Euphausia superba* ||
Class: Malacostracan

Krill are little crustaceans that live in large groups and serve as the primary food source for baleen whales and many other animals.
(See also on p. 86.)

Humpback Whale
|| *Megaptera novaeangliae* ||
Class: Mammal

Humpback whales use their wing-like flippers for turning. The humpback whale jumps completely out of the water and falls onto its back with an enormous splash. Humpback whales are known for their low-frequency song, which can last for days. They spend summers in polar zones, where they find food. (See also on p. 10.)

Blue Whale

Balaenoptera musculus
Class: Mammal

The blue whale is the largest animal in the world (up to 100 feet long!). It has characteristic grooves running along its throat. When blue whales come to the surface to breathe, they spout a stream of water 20 to 30 feet high in the air. They live all over the world—mostly in deep water —except for the Mediterranean, the Red Sea, and the Persian Gulf. (See also on p. 86.)

Emperor Penguin

Aptenodytes forsteri
Class: Bird

The largest of the penguins, this bird lives exclusively at the South Pole and cannot fly. They walk with their fellow penguins and can swim up to 1,300 feet deep using their wings as flippers, looking for food. The emperor penguin is a very sociable animal and lives in colonies of 10,000 to 20,000 couples.

Arctic Tern

Sterna paradisaea
Class: Bird

Twice a year, this bird with a black crown and white cheeks migrates farther than any other bird: up to 50,000 miles. When fishing for food, the Arctic tern hovers before diving in to make its catch. Despite its name, the Arctic tern spends winter in Antarctica. (See also on p. 86.)

Killer Whale, or Orca

Orcinus orca
Class: Mammal

The killer whale is a hunter that roams near beaches looking for penguins or sea lions to attack, stun, and immobilize with its large mouth. (See also on p. 86.)

INDEX

OF ANIMALS

The bold numbers refer
to pages with maps;
plain numbers refer
to pages with information.

A

African Bush Elephant, **49**, 51
African Stonechat, **52**, 54
Alaskan Husky, **xii**, 2
Alpine Marmot, **13**, 15
Alpine Newt, **20**, 23
American Bison, **1**, 3
American Kestrel, **5**, 6, **65**, 66
American Moose, **xii**, 2
Andean Condor, **64**, 67
Anna's Hummingbird, **5**, 6
Ant Beetle, **1**, 3
Appaloosa Horse, **1**, 3
Arabian Camel, **48**, 51
Arctic Fox, **85**, 86
Arctic Tern, **85**, 86, **88**, 91
Ardennes Draft Horse, **12**, 14
Asian Elephant, **36**, 39
Atlantic Bluefin Tuna, **8**, 11, **68**, 70
Atlantic Ghost Crab, **8**, 10
Atlantic Mackerel, **21**, 23, **84**, 87
Atlantic Puffin, **17**, 18, **84**, 86
Atlantic Sailfish, **8**, 11, **69**, 71
Atlantic Salmon, **8**, 11, **69**, 70
Atlas Moth, **41**, 43
Azure Vase Sponge, **9**, 10

B

Baikal Seal, **33**, 34
Bald Eagle, **4**, 7

Banded Sea Krait, **80**, 83
Barn Swallow, **16**, 18, **28**, 30, **53**, 55
Black Grouse, **17**, 19
Black Rhinoceros, **48**, 50
Black Woodpecker, **29**, 31
Black-Blotched Porcupinefish, **80**, 83
Black-Headed Gull, **5**, 6, **29**, 30
Black-Headed Spider Monkey, **60**, 62
Blackbar Triggerfish, **44**, 46, **81**, 83
Blue Tang, **44**, 47
Blue Whale, **84**, 86, **88**, 91
Blue-Winged Grasshopper, **40**, 42
Bohemian Waxwing, **29**, 31
Bornean Orangutan, **36**, 39
Brazilian Porcupine, **60**, 62
Brimstone Butterfly, **29**, 30
Broad-Bodied Chaser, **29**, 31
Brown Bear, **xii**, 2, **24**, 26
Brown Fur Seal, **56**, 58
Brown Pelican, **65**, 66
Brown-Throated Sloth, **60**, 63
Budgerigar, **76**, 79

C

Caribou, **xii**, 2, **24**, 26
Cave Nectar Bat, **41**, 43
Chambered Nautilus, **80**, 82
Chamois, **12**, 14
Channel-Billed Toucan, **64**, 67
Colorado Potato Beetle, **5**, 7
Common Blackbird, **16**, 19
Common Blue Butterfly, **17**, 19
Common Chimpanzee, **48**, 51
Common Cuttlefish, **20**, 23
Common Dolphin, **56**, 59
Common Green Bottle Fly, **17**, 19
Common Hermit Crab, **20**, 22
Common Kingfisher, **16**, 18, **40**, 42
Common Lobster, **20**, 23
Common Octopus, **45**, 46, **56**, 59, **69**, 71
Common Opossum, **1**, 3, **61**, 63
Common Otter, **32**, 34

Common Peafowl, **41**, 42
Common Starfish, **9**, 11
Common Sunstar, **84**, 87
Common Wasp, **77**, 79
Common Wombat, **73**, 75
Crabeater Seal, **89**, 90
Crested Porcupine, **12**, 15
Cross-Cut Carpet Shell, **21**, 23

D

Daubenton's Bat, **16**, 18
Deep-Sea Angler, **80**, 82
Domestic Cow, **13**, 15
Donkey, **72**, 74
Dugong, **56**, 58, **80**, 82
Dyeing Dart Frog, **60**, 62

E

Edible Frog, **20**, 22
Electric Ray, **56**, 59
Emperor Dragonfly, **17**, 19
Emperor Penguin, **88**, 91
Eurasian Blue Tit, **16**, 19
Eurasian Collared Dove, **28**, 31, **40**, 43
Eurasian Lynx, **24**, 27, **37**, 39
Eurasian Oystercatcher, **16**, 19
European Badger, **12**, 14
European Beaver, **20**, 22
European Green Crab, **21**, 22
European Hedgehog, **12**, 14
European Rabbit, **12**, 15, **72**, 74
Ewe, **17**, 19
Eyed Cowry, **57**, 59

F

Fennec Fox, **48**, 50
Fire Salamander, **33**, 35
Flap-Necked Chameleon, **48**, 50

Flying Fish, **44**, 47, **68**, 70
Frilled Lizard, **72**, 74

G

Garden Dormouse, **24**, 27
Giant Anteater, **61**, 63
Giant Manta Ray, **45**, 47
Giant Panda, **37**, 38
Giraffe, **49**, 51
Goat, **24**, 26
Gold Ringer, **57**, 59
Golden Eagle, **4**, 7, **28**, 31
Gray Heron, **40**, 43, **52**, 55
Gray Wolf, **xii**, 2, **24**, 27
Gray's Leaf Insect, **37**, 39
Great Black-Backed Gull, **16**, 18
Great Scallop, **20**, 23
Great Spotted Cuckoo, **15**, 18, **53**, 55
Great White Shark, **8**, 11, **80**, 83
Greater Flamingo, **53**, 54
Green Anaconda, **68**, 71
Green Hairstreak Butterfly, **28**, 31
Green Iguana, **60**, 62
Green Sea Turtle, **69**, 71
Grooved Brain Coral, **8**, 10
Guinea Moray Eel, **44**, 46

H

Hoopoe, **52**, 54
House Fly, **4**, 6, **28**, 31
House Sparrow, **65**, 67
Humpback Whale, **9**, 10, **89**, 90

I

Imperial Shag, **88**, 90

J

Jaguar, **xii**, 3
Jet Ant, **13**, 15

K

Killer Whale, **84**, 86, **88**, 91
Koala, **72**, 75
Krill, **84**, 86, **89**, 90

L

Least Weasel, **1**, 3
Leatherback Sea Turtle, **57**, 59, **80**, 82
Leopard, **37**, 38, **48**, 50
Lined Seahorse, **9**, 11
Lion, **48**, 50
Lioness, **48**, 50
Longnose Butterflyfish, **44**, 47

M

Madagascan Sunset Moth, **52**, 55
Magnificent Sea Anemone, **45**, 46
Mallard, **33**, 34, **77**, 78
Maned Wolf, **60**, 62
Marine Iguana, **68**, 71
Mediterranean Monk Seal, **20**, 23
Meerkat, **48**, 51
Monarch Butterfly, **4**, 6
Mourning Cloak Butterfly, **41**, 42, **76**, 78
Multicolored Asian Ladybug, **41**, 43
Mute Swan, **28**, 31, **77**, 78

N

Narwhal, **32**, 34, **84**, 87
Nile Crocodile, **57**, 58
Nile Perch, **56**, 58

Northern House Mosquito, **5**, 7, **64**, 66
Northern Pike, **20**, 22
Northern Raven, **28**, 30

O

Oarfish, **44**, 46
Omul, **32**, 35
Orange-Tip Butterfly, **17**, 19
Oscellaris Clownfish, **45**, 46
Ostrich, **48**, 51

P

Pacific Oyster, **33**, 34
Pale-Throated Sloth, **61**, 63
Pansy Daggerwing, **64**, 67
Peacock Butterfly, **17**, 19
Peters' Elephantnose Fish, **57**, 58
Plains Zebra, **48**, 51
Platypus, **81**, 82
Polar Bear, **85**, 86
Praying Mantis, **24**, 27
Purple Emperor Butterfly, **40**, 43
Purple-Spotted Swallowtail, **76**, 79
Purple-Striped Jellyfish, **56**, 59

Q

Queen Angelfish, **8**, 10, **68**, 70

R

Raggiana Bird-of-Paradise, **76**, 79
Razor-Billed Auk, **4**, 7, **85**, 87
Red Admiral Butterfly, **4**, 6, **52**, 55
Red Cardinal, **4**, 7
Red Deer, **12**, 14, **25**, 27, **36**, 39
Red Fox, **13**, 15
Red Imported Fire Ant, **36**, 38, **61**, 63, **73**, 75
Red Kangaroo, **73**, 75
Red Lionfish, **81**, 83
Red Sea Bannerfish, **57**, 59
Red Squirrel, **12**, 15
Reindeer, **24**, 26
Ring-Tailed Lemur, **49**, 50
Rock Ptarmigan, **13**, 14, **84**, 86
Réunion Stonechat, **52**, 55

S

Sacred Ibis, **52**, 54
Saltwater Crocodile, **80**, 83
Scarlet Ibis, **64**, 66
Scarlet Macaw, **64**, 67
Sea Fan, **21**, 23
Sea Otter, **32**, 35, **45**, 47
Seven-Spotted Ladybug, **17**, 19
Silkworm Moth, **40**, 43
Silver-Washed Fritillary, **40**, 42
Sloane's Viperfish, **8**, 10, **80**, 82
Smooth Hammerhead Shark, **8**, 11, **44**, 47
Smooth-Fronted Caiman, **68**, 70
Snow Leopard, **25**, 26, **36**, 38
Snowy Owl, **28**, 30, **85**, 87
Southern Giant Petrel, **52**, 55, **88**, 90
Southern Royal Albatross, **65**, 66, **76**, 79
Sperm Whale, **32**, 35, **81**, 82, **84**, 87
Spinner Dolphin, **68**, 70

Springbok, **49**, 51
Stag Beetle, **17**, 19
Stick Insect, **73**, 75
Stone Marten, **24**, 27
Strawberry Poison Frog, **60**, 63
Sulphur-Crested Cockatoo, **76**, 78
Superb Fairy-Wren, **77**, 78

T

Tasmanian Devil, **72**, 74
Three-Spined Stickleback, **20**, 22
Tiger, **25**, 26, **36**, 38
Tokoeka Kiwi, **73**, 75
Tubeworm, **32**, 35
Tufted Gray Langur, **37**, 38

W

Wall Brown Butterfly, **29**, 30
Walrus, **33**, 34, **84**, 87
Western Diamondback Rattlesnake, **xii**, 2
Western Gorilla, **48**, 50
Western Honey Bee, **17**, 19, **76**, 79
Wide-Snouted Sawfish, **44**, 47, **56**, 58
Wild Boar, **12**, 15, **36**, 39, **72**, 74

Y

Yellow-Backed Sunbird, **40**, 42
Yellow-Collared Lovebird, **52**, 54